Lancaster County

PENNSYLVANIA DIVORCES

1786–1832

Eugene F. Throop

HERITAGE BOOKS
2013

HERITAGE BOOKS

AN IMPRINT OF HERITAGE BOOKS, INC.

Books, CDs, and more—Worldwide

For our listing of thousands of titles see our website
at
www.HeritageBooks.com

Published 2013 by
HERITAGE BOOKS, INC.
Publishing Division
100 Railroad Ave. #104
Westminster, Maryland 21157

International Standard Book Numbers
Paperbound: 978-0-7884-0393-4
Clothbound: 978-0-7884-6906-0

CONTENTS

Foreword v

Abbreviations vii

Lancaster County, Pennsylvania, Divorces 1

Surname Index 125

◆   ◆   ◆

FOREWORD

◆   ◆   ◆

For over twenty-six years, I have been involved in genealogical research for others. During that time, it became increasingly apparent that many researchers were overlooking an important aid to their genealogical investigation, and that was the divorce records. Despite the great personal turmoil involved in a divorce case, these records are at times a gold mine of information for family historians. Usually, when a woman filed for a divorce she did so "by her next friend," who often was a close male relative such as a father or brother. Many of the witnesses who testified were neighbors or relatives of the divorcing couple, and their relationships were duly noted.

Having been through a divorce myself, I can certainly attest to the emotional toll it has on all directly affected. I'm sure it was no different in the time period my book covers. Often, these early divorces came as the unavoidable result of very distressing circumstances such as desertion, extreme cruelty, and/or adultery. I noted, also, distinct similarities with modern-day divorces such as vindictive wives trying to take their husbands for all they could, and attorneys who played both ends against the middle to get a huge slice of the "pie."

It was amusing to see the strange spellings which I left as they were originally recorded. Some of the justices of the peace were notorius spellers and some were notorius handwriters. For those stuck on the idea that a surname should be spelled one way only, please note how careless clerks and Justices of the Peace were. I saw instances where the same surname was spelled three different ways on a document written by the same individual!

This compilation of Lancaster County divorces is invaluable, not only for those interested in the history and genealogies of Lancaster County, but many other locations as well. When a husband or wife left their mate, they often went quite a distance.

Hopefully, my readers will forgive me for summarizing most of the records I copied. By doing so, I used fewer pages making it easier to copy and easier to type. I also avoided repeating the same legal terminology over and over. I tried very hard not to miss anything of real value that my readers would want to know.

For those interested in where I obtained my information because they wish to be sure I copied the information correctly or they want a copy of the original record, I will let you know. The earliest divorce records prior to 1810 are on microfilm at the Pennsylvania State Archives in Harrisburg, Pa. The divorce records from 1810 until I stopped transcribing are in the basement of the Lancaster County Historical Society in Lancaster, Pa. From 1850, they are in the Lancaster County Courthouse in Lancaster, Pa.

My sincere thanks go to the personnel at the Lancaster County Historical Society who went out of their way to assist me. They are often very busy, yet, they found time to help everyone which included me! In my opinion, the Lancaster County Historical Society is the most organized historical society I have been in, and we all can be thankful they were instrumental in preserving these records for posterity. I hope all my readers find these records interesting and useful.

Eugene F. Throop

Abstract

♦   ♦   ♦

Abbreviations

♦   ♦   ♦

Adjd. - Adjurned
Apr. - April
atty. - attorney
Aug. - August
Co. - County
contd. - continued
Dec. - December
Esq. - Esquire
Feb. - February
Gen. - General
Jan. - January
Jul. - July
Jun. - June
Jr. - Junior
Mar. - March

Md. - Maryland
N.C. - North Carolina
"N.E.I." - "Non Est Inventus"
N.J. - New Jersey
Nov. - November
Oct. - October
Oh. - Ohio
Pa. - Pennsylvania
prothy. - prothonotary
Rev. - Reverend
S.C. - South Carolina
Sept. - September
Sr. - Senior
Twp. - Township
Va. - Virginia

LANCASTER COUNTY, PENNSYLVANIA DIVORCES

Jul. 19, 1786 - Petition of Esther McCormick. She married at Lebanon in Lancaster Co., Pa., Charles McCormick. As of last Aug. and before he gave himself up to lewd practices and "adulterous conversation and intercource [sic] with lewd woman." He also physically abused her with clubs, sticks and his fists. She considered her life endangered by her husband. She had lived in this state over a year and desires a divorce from her husband.

Feb. 8, 1787 - Petition of Eve Simony by her next friend George Stohler before Joseph Shippen, Jr., justice of the Court of Common Pleas of Lancaster Co., Pa. She had married John Jacob Simony who treated her so cruelly that she was forced to leave him which forced her to depend upon charity "instead of enjoying part of that estate which she by many years of labor helped to earn. That the said John Jacob Simony is a man possessed of a very great estate." Eve Simony signed her petition by mark.

Apr. 15, 1788 - Subpoena to Catharine Wright to appear in court at Philadelphia, Pa., Jul. 2, 1788, to answer her husband's libel for a divorce.

May 22, 1788 - Conviction of Catharine Wright of adultery by a Grand Inquest for the county of Dauphin at a Court of Quarter Sessions before Joseph Montgomery, Esq. She committed adultery Apr. 10, 1787, in Dauphin Co., Pa., with Joseph Keller, yeoman of Dauphin Co., Pa., Both were married as Joseph Keller had a wife named Elizabeth. This act of adultery resulted in a "bastard child." Catharine Wright was sentenced to pay a five pound fine, pay costs of prosecution, "and in the meantime be committed." - Copy extracted from records by Alex. Grayson, clerk.

May 28, 1788 - Petition of Joseph Wright, yeoman before Thomas McKean, justice of the Supreme Court of Pa., for a divorce from his wife, Catharine. He married Sept. 8, 1784, Catharine Link of the borough of Lancaster. "That the said Catharine hath behaved in a very gross and improper manner towards your petitioner, hath frequently eloped and hath ran your petitioner in debt to a considerable sum, which he hath discharged." They separated in Aug. 1785 and since then she had committed adultery of which she was convicted in Dauphin Co., Pa.

Jul. 1, 1788 - Anthony Kelker, Esq., sheriff of Dauphin Co., Pa., testified that he served subpoena on Catharine Wright May 28, 1788. Testified before Thomas McKean, chief justice of the Supreme Court of Pa.

Jul. 15, 1788 - Subpoena to Catharine Wright late of Lancaster Co., Pa., to appear in court at Philadelphia, Pa., Sept. 24, 1788.

Aug. 23, 1788 - Anthony Kelker, Esq., high sheriff of Dauphin Co., Pa., testified he served subpoena on Catharine Wright and left a copy of subpoena Aug. 20, 1788. Testified before J. Kean, justice of the Court of Common Pleas of Dauphin Co., Pa.

Undated - Testimony of Henry Muhlenberg, Lutheran minister at Lancaster, Pa., that he married Joseph Wright of Manor Twp., Lancaster Co., Pa., Sept. 8, 1784, to Catharine Lick of the borough of Lancaster, Pa.

Sept. 24, 1788 - The Supreme Court of Pa., granted Joseph Wright a divorce from his wife, Catharine Wright.

Jun. 12, 1789 - Petition of Susan Wilson before J. Hubley, justice of the Court of Common Pleas, Lancaster Co., Pa. She described herself as "Susan Wilson of Lancaster Co., Pa., Spinster." She married Hugh Wilson, then of Lancaster Co., Pa., Aug. 11, 1762. He frequently beat her and often eloped and deserted her without any of the necessities of life. In Sept. of 1782 he deserted her and never returned to her and he has not wrote her since that time, either. She has no knowledge of where he is. Susan Wilson signed by mark. Notation on the front of this document "22 Decr. 1789 N.C.F."

Apr. 27, 1790 - Petition of John Etter, of Lancaster Co., Pa., yeoman, before Henry Flagle. John Etter was the next friend of Barbara Selser, wife of Michael Selser of York Co., Pa. Barbara married in Hopewell Twp., York Co., Pa., Sept. 1, 1789, Michael Selser. He abused her and was found guilty of assault and battery by the Court of General Quarter Session of York Co., Pa. Earlier he had shot and wounded her "in a most dangerous manner." His treatment forced her to leave "and hath thrown her into the greatest distress and misery." Barbara Selser signed by mark.

May 4, 1790 - William Atlee ordered a subpoena to be issued to Michael Selser to appear before the Supreme Court of Pennsylvania, to answer his wife's charges and petition for a divorce.

Apr. 15, 1791 - Subpoena to Michael Selser of York Co., Pa., to appear before the Supreme Court of Pennsylvania in Philadelphia, Pa., Jul. 1791. Conrad Laub, sheriff, reported that he properly served the subpoena on Michael Selser.

Oct. 19, 1790 - Subpoena to James Harris late of Lower Paxton Twp., Dauphin Co., Pa., to appear before the Supreme Court of Pennsylvania at Philadelphia, Pa., Jan. 3, 1791, to answer his wife's libel for a divorce. (Note - why the subpoena is dated before the petition is a mystery to me!)

Nov. 17, 1790 - Petition of Jane Harris by her next friend Robert Clark. She married May 23, 1791, James Harris of Lower Paxton Twp. then Lancaster Co., Pa., now Dauphin Co., Pa. Shortly after their marriage he "gave himself up to dissolute and idle courses." In the latter end of Nov. 1791 he deserted her. Soon afterward she had a child and her husband made no provision for her. She hath frequently wrote her husband inviting him to return but he never has nor told her he would provide for her "as a good husband ought to do." Her husband's father has informed her by letter that James Harris lives in N.C. with another woman as his wife and has several children reputed to be his.

Dec. 6, 1790 - James Clunie, sheriff, testified that he could not find James Harris in Dauphin Co., Pa., and left a copy of the subpoena at his last abode in Dauphin Co., Pa., at the house of Michael Frantz on Nov. 29, 1791.

Apr. 15, 1791 - Court appoints Joseph Montgomery, Esq., and Alexander Grayson, Esq., of Harrisburg, Pa., to take depositions in the case of James Harris vs. Jane Harris.

Apr. 15, 1791 - Subpoena issued to James Harris late of Lower Paxton Twp., Dauphin Co., Pa., to appear before the Supreme Court Jul. 2, 1791, at Philadelphia, Pa., to show cause why his wife Jane Harris should not have a divorce from him.

May 20, 1791 - John McCleary swears he could not find James Harris in Dauphin Co., Pa., and left a copy of the subpoena at the dwelling house of Michael Frantz his last place of abode there May 16, 1791.

May 27, 1791 - Deposition of James Colier of Paxton Twp., Dauphin Co., Pa., held at the house of Samuel Grahams, innholder at the Sign of the Federal Arms in the borough of Harrisburg. He had known Jane Harris since he was six years of age and her husband James Harris since about the time of his marriage to Jane. Jane was formerly Jane Hutchison and she married James Harris in her mother's house in Paxton Twp. about the middle of May 1779. He "saw them married and put to bed together and that they lived some months together at the house of her mother as man and wife." James Harris left his wife "with child" at her mother's house. He didn't know why he left or where he went. He has not seen James Harris since but he had seen a letter he sent his wife about two years ago. He said he resided in S.C. and he expected to see her in a few months. The letter was not dated and he didn't recollect what place in S.C. it was from. He had also heard that James Harris lives in S.C. with another woman. He wrote a letter back to James Harris for his wife in answer. He wrote it for her at her insistence directed to the father of the said James Harris requesting him to forward it to his son in which "letter she desired him to return and upbraided him with his inconstancy [sic] and neglect and told him of her own faithfulness to her marriage tye [sic]." He knows of no provision made by James Harris for his wife and child nor of any invitation made by him for his wife to "cohabit with him."

May 27, 1791 - Deposition of Richard Fulton of Paxton Twp., Dauphin Co., Pa., - aged 27 years. He had known Jane Harris, formerly Jane Hutchison, about 14 years and James Harris about 12 years ago. He was not present at their marriage but saw them at meeting together and knew they were regarded as man and wife. He knew James deserted his pregnant wife and about six months later "she was delivered of a female child." He doesn't know why he left unless it was because he was in debt and has heard he went to S.C. with another woman. He has heard Jane Harris declare she had written to her husband and has always understood it was her wish that he should return to her. He knows of no provision made by James Harris for his wife nor "does not know that the said James Harris hath refused to return and live with the said Jane."

May 28, 1791 - Deposition of Rev. John Elder, minister of the Gosepel in the congregation of Paxton, Dauphin Co., Pa., aged 81 years. He knew Jane Harris since she was a child and knew James Harris about 2 months prior to their marriage. Jane was Jane Hutchison and she married James Harris at her brother's house where her mother also lived May 27, 1779. They lived together there about seven or eight months. In the fall of 1779 James deserted his wife and shortly thereafter she had a child. He believed "he left her on account of his being much in debt and that it was said he went to Virginia and from there to South Carolina." To the best of his knowledge James has never returned to Pa., but he has heard he lives in either N.C., or S.C., with another woman not his wife. He believes James Harris left no provision for his wife and child. Jane Harris informed him "that she had received a letter from the father of the said James giving her to understand she had nothing to expect from her said husband as he was married to and living with another woman."

Jul. 2, 1791 - James Clunie, sheriff of Dauphin Co., Pa., testified he made public proclamation at Dauphin Co., Pa., courthouse three, several days in May 1791 term for the appearance of James Harris.

Jul. 2, 1791 - James Ash, sheriff of Philadelphia Co., Pa., testified he published notice for the appearance of James Harris in *Dunlap's American Daily Advertiser* and *Halls & Sellers Gazette* and made public declaration at three market days at the old courthouse and in open court.

Undated - Supreme Court of Pennsylvania, granted Jane Harris a divorce from James Harris.

Sept. 15, 1792 - Subpoena to John Zuber of Lancaster Co., Pa., to appear in Court at Philadelphia, Pa., Jan. 7, 1793, to answer the libel of his wife, Juliana Zuber for a divorce.

Oct. 23, 1792 - Petition of Juliana Zuber before J. Yeates, judge of the Supreme Court of Pennsylvania, by her next friend, Henry Stauffer. She married John Zuber in Aug. of 1784. He "behaved himself in a very improper manner" and deserted her over seven years ago. She signed her petition "by mark."

Dec. 19, 1792 - Juliana Zuber testified that she left a copy of the subpoena at the house of John Beixler in Brecknock Twp., Lancaster Co., Pa., the last abode of John Zuber who "cannot be found." She testified this before Jasper Yeates, judge of the Supreme Court of Pennsylvania.

Jan. 7, 1793 - Subpoena to John Zuber of Lancaster Co., Pa., to appear before the Supreme Court of Pennsylvania, in Philadelphia, Pa., Apr. 1, 1793, to answer the libel of his wife Juliana Zuber for a divorce.

Mar. 20, 1793 - Juliana Zuber testified that she left a copy of the subpoena Mar. 6, 1793, at the house of Abraham Beixler in Brecknock Twp., Lancaster Co., Pa., the last abode of John Zuber. She could not find out any information as to where he went. She testified before J. Hubley, justice of the peace, and signed "by mark."

Apr. 1, 1793 - Supreme Court of Pennsylvania, appointed Frederick Kuhn and Paul Zantinger, both of the borough of Lancaster, Pa., to take depositions in this case.

Apr. 1, 1793 - Subpoena to John Zuber of Lancaster Co., Pa., to appear before the Supreme Court of Pennsylvania, at Philadelphia, Pa., Sept. 2, 1793, to answer the libel of his wife, Juliana Zuber for a divorce.

Jul. 2, 1793 - Deposition of John Painter who testified he knows John Zuber well but not where he now lives. Five years ago last Aug. or Sept. John Zuber left his wife and left Lancaster Co., Pa., John Zuber "appeared extravigant and frolicksome and when his father-in-law would not maintain him he absconded." He lived ten miles from John Zuber and Juliana Zuber.

Jul. 2, 1793 - Deposition of Martin Heller who knew John Zuber well. His last place of abode was in Brecknock Twp. in the co. of Lancaster where he and his brother-in-law, Abraham Beixler, rented his father's place from the executors. Abraham Beixler kept house and John Zuber boarded with him. Five years ago next fall John Zuber left his wife and never returned. He was told by Emanuel Carpenter that he had heard that John Zuber was married in Kentucky.

Jul. 2, 1793 - Deposition of Andrew Rudy who knew John Zuber and that he lived at his father's place. Five years ago next fall John Zuber left his wife and never returned to her.

Undated - Supreme Court of Pennsylvania, granted Juliana Zuber a divorce from her husband John Zuber.

Mar. 3, 1794 - Petition of Cornelius Mayer of Manheim Twp., Lancaster Co., Pa., yeoman, said he married Nov. 1, 1791, Catharine Kendrick of Conostogoe Twp., Lancaster Co., Pa. She frequently eloped from him and she left him for good in May of 1793 and has committed adultery and continues to do so.

Apr. 19, 1794 - Subpoena to Catharine Mayer, wife of Cornelius Mayer of Manheim Twp., Lancaster Co., Pa., to appear before the Supreme Court of Pennsylvania, at Philadelphia, Pa., Sept. 1, 1794, to answer the libel of her husband, Cornelius Mayer for a divorce. On the front of this document John Miller, sheriff, testified that he had served the subpoena.

Jan. 24, 1795 - The Supreme Court of Pennsylvania, appointed John Hubley of the borough of Lancaster, Pa., to take depositions in this case.

Jan. 25, 1795 - Subpoena to Catharine Mayer, wife of Cornelius Mayer of Manheim Twp., Lancaster Co., Pa., to appear in Philadelphia, Pa., before the Supreme Court of Pennsylvania, to answer the libel of her husband, Cornelius Mayer for a divorce.

Apr. 7, 1795 - John Miller, sheriff, testified that he served the above subpoena on Catharine Mayer.

Apr. 13, 1795 - Deposition of Michael App. He knew both parties to this case and was present at their wedding at his own house and seen them married by Rev. Henry Muchlenberg.

Apr. 13, 1795 - Deposition of William Pain who knew both parties to this case for many years. They lived together "better than three months." She left her husband and married Samuel Sites and had one child by him and is pregnant with another. William Pain signed "by mark."

Apr. 13, 1795 - Deposition of Susannah Paine who said she knew both parties to this case and they lived together about three months as man and wife. Catharine Mayer left her husband and married Samuel Sites and had one child by him and was pregnant with another. She signed her deposition "by mark."

Sept. 7, 1795 - The Supreme Court of Pennsylvania, granted Cornelius Mayer a divorce from his wife, Catharine Mayer.

Feb. 1, 1786 - Marriage license for Philip Adam Shreiner of Manheim Twp., Lancaster Co., Pa., yeoman, to marry Elizabeth Singhaas of Donegal Twp., Lancaster Co., Pa.

Jun. 10, 1793 - Petition of Philip Shriner of Newberry Twp., York Co., Pa., that he married Jan. 31, 1786, Elizabeth Singhaas, the daughter of Casper Singhaas of Mount Joy Twp., Lancaster Co., Pa. They had three children Catharine, Michael, and Elizabeth all since dead. Over a year ago she abandoned him without any reasonable cause. She has since committed adultery with Joseph Watkins and married him in May of 1794. They now live in Northumberland Co., Pa.

Oct. 20, 1794 - John Hubley, Esq., clerk of Court of Quarter Sessions in Lancaster Co., Pa., testified that Philip Adam Shreiner took out a license to marry Elizabeth Singhaas Feb. 1, 1786.

Oct. 21, 1794 - Deposition of David Hammond, Esq., that he married in May or Jun. of 1793 a woman calling herself Elizabeth Singhorse [sic] to a man calling himself Joseph Watkins.

Jul. 26, 1795 - Favel Roan, Esq., late sheriff of Northumberland Co., Pa., testified that he served a subpoena on Elizabeth Shreiner by leaving her a copy more than fifteen days before she was due to appear in court.

Sept. 13, 1795 - Supreme Court of Pennsylvania, appointed William Wilson, John Thornburg, and Walter Clark to take depositions in this case.

Oct. 25, 1795 - Henry Muhlenberg, minister at Lancaster, Pa., testified that he married Philip Adam Shreiner of Manheim Twp., Lancaster Co., Pa., yeoman, to Elizabeth Singhaas of Donegal Twp., Lancaster Co., Pa., Feb. 1, 1786.

Oct. 25, 1795 - Deposition of Abel Person that a woman known as Elizabeth Singhaas was married to Joseph Watkins in Turbot Twp., Northumberland Co., Pa., by David Hammond, Esq., last May or Jun. He also said that they have continued to live together as man and wife in Turbot Twp., Northumberland Co., Pa. He has also heard Elizabeth say that she was formerly married to a Philip Shreiner and that they had lived together as man and wife in Newberry Twp., York Co., Pa.

Oct. 25, 1795 - Robert Chambers gave a deposition stating that he knew Philip and Elizabeth Schreiner [sic] when they lived together as man and wife in Newbury Twp., York Co., Pa. He knows that she left her husband in Apr. of 1794. He has often heard Elizabeth say that she is a daughter of Casper Singhaas of Lancaster Co., Pa. Robert Chambers signed his deposition "by mark."

Apr. 9, 1796 - The Supreme Court of Pennsylvania, granted Philip Shriner a divorce from his wife Elizabeth Shriner.

Sept. 13, 1794 - Supreme Court of Pennsylvania, appointed Paul Zantzinger and Jacob Graeff, Esq., of the borough of Lancaster, Pa., to be Commissioners in the case of Eliza. Gamble vs. James Gamble, libel in divorce.

Dec. 5, 1794 - Subpoena to Martha Gamble [sic] to appear in Philadelphia, Pa., before the Supreme Court of Pennsylvania, to answer the libel of her husband, James Gamble for a divorce on Jan. 5, 1795.

Dec. 6, 1794 - John Baker, sheriff, gave a proclamation to Martha Gamble to appear before the Supreme Court of Pennsylvania, Jan. 5,

1795, at Philadelphia, Pa., to answer her husband's libel for a divorce. Proclamation made at Courthouse on Market Street Dec. 10, 1794, Dec. 17, 1794, and Dec. 20, 1794.

Jan. 14, 1795 - Deposition of James Greer who was well acquainted with both parties of this case. Eliza. Gamble left her husband, James Gamble, in Dec. 1789 and went to Ireland and never returned. He heard her say "sometime before she went to Ireland that she would no go and remain with her husband."

Jan. 16, 1795 - Michael App, sheriff of Lancaster Co., Pa., testified Elizabeth Gamble was not in his bailiwick. He had made three days proclamation at the courthouse for her to appear in court.

Apr. 8, 1795 - Deposition of Col. James Morrison who was well acquainted with both parties in this case. He knew Elizabeth Gamble left her husband five years ago last fall and has remained separate ever since. She first left him seven or eight years ago but then returned. He heard her say she would not stay in this country but would leave her husband and return to Ireland. He testified that he accompanied her as far as New Castle and that she appeared determined to go on alone to Ireland.

Apr. 8, 1795 - Deposition of William White who knew that Elizabeth Gamble left her husband five years ago last Dec. He also testified that two or three years before that she left her husband and went to New Castle with the intention of going to Ireland but she returned. He had heard her say "that she did not like this country and would not live or stay in it."

Sept. 15, 1798 - Subpoena from the Supreme Court of Pennsylvania, to James McCoy, late of Cecil Co., Md., to appear before the Supreme Court of Pennsylvania, in Philadelphia, Pa., Dec. 29, 1798.

Dec. 3, 1798 - Petition of Isabella McCoy by her next friend Hugh McEntire. She married James McCoy of Cecil Co., Md., in Dec. of 1792. Since their marriage they resided with her father William McEntire in Lancaster Co., Pa., until Mar. of 1793 when he went to Cecil Co., Md. for three months. He then returned to her and they lived together until Mar. 1, 1794, when he again left her at her father's house and went to Cecil Co., Md., and remained a year. He then returned to her father's house in Lancaster Co., Pa., and they lived together until Sept. of 1795. Then after beating and abusing her he left until Jun. of 1797 at which time he came back and promised to treat her well and took her to Cecil Co., Md., where they lived together until Feb. of 1798. During that period her husband "abused her and treated her in a very barbarous and cruel manner -in dragging her by the hair through the house and whipping her with great severity with a cowskin." He then took her back to her father and a few days later wrote her father that he was not to send her back as he was determined never to live with her again.

Dec. 8, 1798 - Alexander Scott testified before George McCullough, justice of the peace in Lancaster Co., Pa., that he served the subpoena on James McCoy to appear before the Supreme Court of Pennsylvania, in Philadelphia, Pa., to answer the libel of his wife for a divorce.

Dec. 29, 1798 - The Supreme Court of Pennsylvania, made it's decision that the Libellant only came to this state within seven or eight months and was not eligible for a divorce because her residence in the state of Pennsylvania, was less than a year.

Feb. 24, 1795 - Subpoena from the Supreme Court of Pennsylvania, to Dorothea Waggoner to appear before the Supreme Court of Pennsylvania, in Philadelphia, Pa., Apr. 6, 1795, to answer the libel of her husband, George Waggoner for a divorce.

Feb. 24, 1795 - Court of Oyer and Terminer and General Jail Delivery of Lancaster Co., Pa. Inquest convicted Dorothea Waggoner of Mannor [sic] Twp. who committed adultery with James Albright Jan. 1, 1795. She admitted guilt and was sentenced to pay a fine of five pounds and spend one month in Lancaster Co., Pa., Jail and pay costs of her prosecution. Jury consisted of James Crawford, Frederick Stineman, Frederick Frick, Jacob Stufft, Christopher Hager, Henry Bennett, Philip Dean, Thomas Turner, Henry Gross, Henry Locher, Henry Witmer, John Brinkley, Daniel Lefever, Michael Kreider, Jacob Bear, Christian Stauffer, John Myer, and Michael Forner.

Feb. 28, 1795 - Petition of George Waggonner of Lancaster Co., Pa. He had married Feb. 26, 1775, Dorothea Foulke of Conestogoe Twp., Lancaster Co., Pa. She left him about six months ago and committed adultery, of which she was convicted at a Court of Oyer and Terminer held at Lancaster, Pa., last Monday in Feb. of 1795.

Apr. 3, 1795 - George Wagner [sic] appeared before the Supreme Court of Pennsylvania, and testified that he served a copy of the subpoena on his wife Feb. 28, 1795, in the borough of Lancaster, Pa.

Apr. 16, 1795 - Subpoena from the Supreme Court of Pennsylvania, to Dorothea Waggoner to appear before the Supreme Court of Pennsylvania, in Philadelphia, Pa., Sept. 7, 1795, to answer the libel of her husband for a divorce.

Aug. 5, 1795 - George Waggoner testified before the Supreme Court of Pennsylvania, that he served the subpoena on his wife Jul. 25, 1795.

Sept. 7, 1795 - Supreme Court of Pennsylvania, granted the divorce.

Apr. 18, 1795 - Subpeona from the Supreme Court of Pennsylvania, to John Henry of the borough of Lancaster, Pa., to appear before the Supreme Court of Pennsylvania, in Philadelphia, Sept. 7, 1795, to answer the libel of his wife, Agnes Henry, by her next friend, James Thompson. Subpoena was served Jul. 13, 1795, by Michael App, sheriff.

May 29, 1795 - Petition of Agnes Henry by her next friend James Thompson. She married Nov. 18, 1792, John Henry. Her husband committed adultery with Esther Jenkins in Lancaster Co., Pa., between Jul. 1, 1794, and Aug. 10, 1794. He was convicted of this in the May session of court in 1795.

Jun. 18, 1795 - Aug. Sessions 1795 Lancaster Co., Pa., Quarter Sessions Grand Inquest. John Henry of Lancaster Borough was accused of common adultery with Esther Jenkins on Aug. 6, 1794. Jury of twelve men declared him guilty (Abraham Hauffman, Benjamin Shaum, Jonas Metzgar, Jacob Bakestose, John Reist, Martin Streiner, Andrew Leibly, Martin Jordan, John Ulerich, Frederick Siventzell, John Karch, and John Hagey). He was sentenced to pay a fine of fifty pounds, spend nine months in the "goal of Lancaster County" and pay the cost of his prosecution. Signed by John Hubley, Esq., clerk of the Court of Quarter Sessions Lancaster Co., Pa.

Sept. 19, 1795 - Subpoena from the Supreme Court of Pennsylvania, to John Henry of the borough of Lancaster, Pa., to appear in Court at Philadelphia, Pa., Dec. 14, 1794, to answer the libel of his wife, Agnes Henry. Served by Michael App, sheriff, Nov. 10, 1795, between the hours of 9 a.m. and 10 a.m.

Undated - Rev. Elisha Rigg, rector of St. James Church in Lancaster, Pa., testified that he married John Henry and Agnes Readeck at Lancaster, Pa., Nov. 18, 1792.

Dec. 14, 1795 - The Supreme Court of Pennsylvania, granted Agnes Henry a divorce from her husband, John Henry.

Dec. 25, 1796 - Petition of Ann Long by her next friend, Hugh Miller, before Frederick Kuhn, judge of the Court of Common Pleas of Lancaster Co., Pa. She had married David Long and he "wilfully and maliciously deserted" her over eight years ago and she didn't know where he was.

Dec. 31, 1796 - The Supreme Court of Pennsylvania, issued a subpoena to David Long, late of Lancaster Co., Pa., to appear before the Supreme Court of Pennsylvania, in Philadelphia, Pa., the third Monday of Mar. 1797, to answer the libel of his wife, Ann Long for a divorce.

Mar. 1797 - Michael App, sheriff of Lancaster Co., Pa., testified he left a copy of the subpoena at the last place of abode of David Long Feb. 11, 1797.

Apr. 1, 1798 - The Supreme Court of Pennsylvania, issued a subpoena to David Long, late of Lancaster Co., Pa., to appear before the Supreme Court of Pennsylvania, at Philadelphia, Pa., the first Monday of Sept. 1798.

Aug. 31, 1798 - Michael App, sheriff of Lancaster Co., Pa., testified that he left a copy of the subpoena at the residence of David Long and submitted his bill for one mile of travel.

Sept. 4, 1798 - The Supreme Court of Pennsylvania, appointed

John Hubley of the borough of Lancaster, Pa., to take depositions in this case.

Feb. 28, 1799 - Deposition of Beershebe Colverman who knew Ann Long all her life and David Long about twenty years. Ann Long was a native of Pa., and had always lived there. David Long and Ann Long lived together as man and wife about four years during which time she was often at their house, sometimes for several months at a time. They appeared happy and contented with each other. In 1787 or 1788, David Long left his wife with declared intention of returning shortly. Several months later he did return for four days and then went away again and never returned. Ann Long always treated her husband tenderly and affectionately and was severely "uneasy and troubled" at his absence. She has heard that David Long went to the vicinity of Fort Pitt and for about four years has heard he is living with another woman. Ann Long has "behaved herself well" since her husband's desertion eleven years ago.

Mar. 21, 1797 - Petition of John Herr of Manor Twp., Lancaster Co., Pa., who married his present wife, Elizabeth, Oct. 10, 1792. She deserted him Mar. 16, 1793, without any just or reasonable cause. Sworn before Frederick Kuhn, assistant judge of Lancaster Co., Pa. John Herr signed his petition in German script.

Apr. 1, 1797 - Supreme Court of Pennsylvania, issued a subpoena to Elizabeth Herr, late of Manor Twp., Lancaster Co., Pa., to appear before the Supreme Court of Pennsylvania, at Philadelphia, Pa., on the first Monday of Sept., 1797, to answer the libel of her husband, John Herr, for a divorce. Michael Rinz, substitute sheriff, testified that he served a copy of this subpoena on Elizabeth Herr Jul. 1, 1797. Distance was three miles to serve the subpoena.

Sept. 16, 1797 - Supreme Court of Pennsylvania, issued a subpoena to Elizabeth Herr to appear before the Supreme Court of Pennsylvania, in Philadelphia, Pa., on the second Monday of Dec. 1797, to answer the libel of her husband, John Herr, for a divorce. Subpoena was served on Elizabeth Herr Nov. 29, 1797, by Christian Carpenter.

Mar. 30, 1798 - Answer of Elizabeth Herr to the libel of her husband, John Herr, filed. She denied all charges of her husband except the fact that they were indeed married.

Dec. 28, 1799 -Supreme Court of Pennsylvania, issued a subpoena to Samuel Leamon, late of Lancaster Co., Pa., to appear before the Supreme Court of Pennsylvania, in Philadelphia, Pa., on the third Monday of Mar., 1800, to answer the libel of his wife, Catharine Leamon, for a divorce.

Jan. 20, 1800 - Petition of Catharine Leamon, late Catharine Roland, by her next friend, John Roland. She is a native of Lancaster Co., Pa. About eight years ago she married Samuel Leamon of

Lancaster Co., Pa. Over four years ago he deserted her without any just cause, leaving her to support their two children. She doesn't known where he now is.

Feb. 25, 1800 - John Roland testified that he left a copy of subpoena on the door of house formerly occupied by Samuel Leaman in New Holland, Lancaster Co., Pa. This house is now vacant as Samuel Leamon left the state and his residence is unknown. Also left a copy of subpoena at the house of Jonathan Roland in New Holland, the last place he resided before that.

Mar. 17, 1800 - Supreme Court of Pennsylvania, issued a subpoena to Samuel Leamon to appear before the Supreme Court of Pennsylvania, in Philadelphia, Pa., on the first Monday of Sept. 1800, to answer the libel of his wife for a divorce. Christian Carpenter, Jr., sheriff of Lancaster Co., Pa., testified that Samuel Leamon was not in Lancaster Co., Pa., and he had made public proclamation on three days in 1800 at the Court of Quarter Sessions for Samuel Leamon to appear in court in Sept. of 1800.

Jul. 30, 1800 - Deposition of Frederick Seger, Esq., of the village of New Holland in Lancaster Co., Pa., before Frederick Kahn and John Hubley. He had known Catharine Leamon since she was about five years of age and she was always decent and respectable. About nine years ago she married Samuel Leamon, being then about seventeen years of age, without her father's consent. As far as he could observe she was an affectionate, good and faithful wife. Samuel Leamon abandoned her Jan. 1, 1796, and left the country, "considerably in debt, and left no support or maintenace for his wife the plaintiff in the said libel, nor has he since supported or maintained her." He doesn't know where it is but he has heard he was seen in "Kentuckee" and also heard it confidently reported that he was dead.

Jul. 30, 1800 - Deposition of Peter Diller of the borough of Lancaster, Pa., who knew both of the parties in this case. He married them out of her father's house and without her father's consent when she was under age. "That during her cohabitation with him she always behaved to him as a faithful and affectionate wife; and has always had the character of a virteous [sic] and respectable girl and still maintans the same." Samuel Leamon left his wife Jan. 1, 1796, without any cause he has heard of. He made no provision for her. He has heard he went to "Kentuckee" but only knows for sure he never returned to Pa. Since his desertion she has lived and been maintained by her father, Jonathan Roland of New Holland.

Aug. 9, 1800 - Jonathan Penrose, sheriff of Philadelphia Co. and City, testified that he made public declaration at the old Courthouse on three days May 17, 28, and 31; also in Court of Common Pleas on Jun. 3, 4, and 17 also in the City Hall and also in public newspapers for one month and upwards for Samuel Leamon to appear before the Supreme Court of Pennsylvania, to answer the libel of his wife,

Catharine Leamon, for a divorce.

Sept. 2, 1800 - The Supreme Court of Pennsylvania, granted Catharine Leamon a divorce from her husband, Samuel Leamon.

Apr. 22, 1800 - Petition of Jane Long of Dunmore Twp., Lancaster Co., Pa., by her next friend, John McConnell, before Robert King, justice of the peace of Lancaster Co., Pa. She married about eight years ago John Long. About five months later he deserted her without any just cause.

Dec. 27, 1800 - Supreme Court of Pennsylvania, issued a subpoena to John Long, late of Lancaster Co., Pa., to appear before the Supreme Court of Pennsylvania, at Philadelphia, Pa., on the third Monday of Mar. 1801 to answer the libel of his wife Jane Long for a divorce.

Mar. 10, 1801 - Michael Rine, sheriff of Lancaster Co., Pa., testified that he left a copy of the subpoena at the house of Robert Long, deceased in Dunmore Twp., Lancaster Co., Pa., Mar. 1, 1801, that being the last place of residence of John Long in Lancaster Co., Pa.

Sept. 19, 1801 - The Supreme Court of Pennsylvania, issued a subpoena to John Long, late of Lancaster Co., Pa., to appear before the Supreme Court of Pennsylvania, at Philadelphia, Pa., on Jan. 2, 1802, to answer the libel of his wife, Jane Long, for a divorce.

Dec. 20, 1801 - Michael Rine, sheriff of Lancaster Co., Pa., left copy of subpoena at late dwelling house of Robert Long, deceased, it being the last abode of John Long on Dec. 9, 1801, and made public proclamation on three different days for his appearance in court to answer the libel of his wife, Jane Long, for a divorce.

Mar. 23, 1801 - Supreme Court of Pennsylvania, appointed Adam Reigart, Jr. and Jacob Graff, Esq., to take depositions in this case.

Undated - Deposition of Robert King, Esq., who knew both parties in this case. He knew they were married in 1790. In the spring of 1791 John Long deserted his wife without any reasonable cause he knew of. He told him that he was determined never to live with her. His wife, Jane Long, is a near neighbor of him and is generally esteemed in the neighborhood and has conducted herself with prudence and decency.

Undated - Deposition of James Morrison who knew both parties in this case. They were married at least nine or ten years ago. About six or seven months after the marriage he deserted his wife without any just cause and has continued absent from her. She is generally respected in the neighborhood where she resides.

Dec. 29, 1801 - The Supreme Court of Pennsylvania, granted Jane Long a divorce from her husband, John Long.

Jan. 2, 1802 - Israel Israel, high sheriff of the county and city of Philadelphia testified that he made public proclamation at the old courthouse three days during the Dec. Term and also in a public newspaper for the appearance of John Long to answer the libel of his wife Jane Long for a divorce.

Sept. 19, 1801 - The Supreme Court of Pennsylvania, issued a subpoena to Barbara Mayer to appear before them at Philadelphia, Pa., on the second Monday of Dec. 1801 to answer the libel of her husband, Rudolph Mayer, for a divorce.

Oct. 13, 1801 - Petition of Rudolph Myer [sic] of Somerset Co., Pa., who married his present wife Barbara in May of 1776 and they lived together fourteen years. Barbara "for a considerable time past has given herself up to adulterous practices."

Dec. 14, 1801 - John Mayer testified he served the subpoena on Barbara Mayer on or before Nov. 23, 1801, for her to appear before the Supreme Court of Pennsylvania, at Philadelphia, Pa., on the second Monday of Dec. 1801 to answer her husband's libel for a divorce.

Dec. 14, 1801 - The Supreme Court of Pennsylvania, issued a subpoena to Barbara Mayer to appear before the Supreme Court of Pennsylvania, to appear there at Philadelphia, Pa., on the third Monday of Mar. in 1802 to answer the libel of her husband for a divorce.

Dec. 15, 1801 - The Supreme Court of Pennsylvania, appointed John Tome and John Gloninger to take depositions in this case.

Dec. 23, 1801 - Jacob Mayer of Dauphin Co., Pa., testified that he knew John Mayer since infancy and became acquainted with Barbara Mayer at her father's house in Heidleburg Twp., Lancaster Co., Pa., and at her brother-in-law John Mayer's house in Heidleburg Twp., Lancaster Co., Pa., about two years before the marriage of John and Barbara Mayer. He was present at their wedding about twenty-six years ago in the Mennonite meetinghouse in Lebanon Twp., then in Lancaster Co., by Frederick Kauffman a Mennonite minister, since deceased. They lived as man and wife about fourteen or fifteen years. It was "common report" and "generally believed" that Barbara Mayer committed adultery with Benjamin Young of Heidleburg Twp., now in Dauphin Co., Pa. Barbara Mayer deserted her husband about eleven or twelve years ago when they lived in York Co., Pa., and eloped without any just cause.

Dec. 23, 1801 - Deposition of Henry Mayer of Lebanon Twp., Dauphin Co., Pa., farmer. He had known John Mayer since infancy and had known Barbara Mayer about two years before her marriage while she lived in her father's house. They were married about twenty-six years ago by Frederick Kauffman, since deceased, in Mennonite meetinghouse and lived as man and wife about fifteen years. It was commonly believed that Barbara Mayer had committed adultery with Benjamin Young "as she herself had made oath thereof before a Justice of the Peace as he this affirmant is informed." About eight or nine years ago, Barbara Mayer told him that she was married to Frederick Fuhrman. About two months later he was at Frederick Fuhrman's house and noted that they lived together. She left John Mayer about eleven years ago while they lived in York Co., Pa.

Dec. 23, 1801 - Deposition of John Shenk of Heidleburg Twp., Dauphin Co., Pa., miller. He had known John Mayer since infancy and Barbara Mayer shortly before her marriage to John Mayer. He was present at their wedding about twenty-five or twenty-six years ago in Mennonite meetinghouse in Lebanon Twp. by Frederick Kauffman. They lived together fourteen or fifteen years. After Barbara Mayer left her husband she had a child and Benjamin Young was reported to be the father.

Dec. 24, 1801 - Deposition of George Hoke of Warwick Twp., York Co., Pa., farmer. He "is little acquainted with the Libellant, that he has been acquainted with the defendant about seven or eight years." Barbara Mayer told him that her daughter living with her was the daughter of Benjamin Young. He knows this girl and she is about eleven or twelve years old. He also knows Frederick Fuhrman and he "further told this affirmant that he Fuhrman did sleep with her the Deponent and he would sleep with her if Rudolph Mayer was present." Frederick Fuhrman and Barbara Mayer have lived together in his neighborhood about three years just as if they were man and wife.

Dec. 24, 1801 - Deposition of Henry Sheffer, Esq., of Heidleburg Twp., Dauphin Co., Pa. He knew John Mayer about twenty years and Barbara Mayer since she was a child and lived with her father who was a near neighbor of his. John and Barbara Mayer lived together about fourteen or fifteen years. About ten or eleven years ago Barbara Mayer made oath before him that she had a bastard child and the father of the child was Benjamin Young of Heidleburg Twp. He issued a warrant and as he understood the affair was settled at the time she pressed charges against Benjamin Young, her husband, lived in York Co., Pa. He knows that Frederick Fuhrman and Barbara Mayer have lived together as if they were man and wife for seven or eight years.

Mar. 15, 1802 - The Supreme Court of Pennsylvania, granted Rudolph Mayer a divorce from his wife, Barbara Mayer.

Mar. 25, 1802 - Abraham Mayer, farmer of Dauphin Co., Pa., testified that he had served the subpoena on Barbara Mayer Feb. 20, 1802, for her to appear in court to answer the libel of her husband, Rudolph Mayer, for a divorce.

Aug. 4, 1802 - Petition of Ann Crawford by her next friend, Gehardus Conwell. She married May 13, 1799, John Crawford who has for a considerable time given himself up to adulterous practices.

Mar. 27, 1802 - Supreme Court of Pennsylvania, issued a subpoena to John Crawford to appear before the Supreme Court of

Pennsylvania, at Philadelphia, Pa., to answer the libel of his wife, Ann Crawford, for a divorce on the first Monday of Sept. 1802.

Mar. 27, 1802 - The Supreme Court of Pennsylvania, issued a subpoena to John Crawford to appear before the Supreme Court of Pennsylvania, in Philadelphia, Pa., on the first Monday of Sept. 1802 to answer the libel of his wife, Ann Crawford, for a divorce.

Aug. 9, 1802 - A copy of the subpoena to John Crawford to appear before the Supreme Court of Pennsylvania, in Philadelphia, Pa., the first Monday of Sept. 1802 was served on him.

Sept. 4, 1802 - Petition of John Crawford that he was issued a subpoena dated Mar. 27, 1802, to appear before the Supreme Court of Pennsylvania, on the first Monday of Sept. 1802 to show cause why his wife Ann should not have a divorce. He stated that he married his present wife, Ann, in Jun. of 1799 in Lancaster Co., Pa. In that same year he was convicted of conterfeiting money and sentenced to twelve years in prison. He is now in prison in Philadelphia, Pa., and unable to attend court and has no money to employ counsel. He asks for a delay to next term to allow him to collect evidence to show she is not bringing this libel of her own accord. He claimed that her pretended friends kept his wife from visiting him and induced her to file for divorce. He possesses a large property and these friends hope to somehow benefit from the divorce action.

Sept. 18, 1802 - The Supreme Court of Pennsylvania, issued a subpoena for John Crawford to appear before the Supreme Court of Pennsylvania, at Philadelphia, Pa., on the first day of Jan. 1803 to answer the libel of his wife, Ann Crawford, for a divorce.

Dec. 28, 1802 - Deposition of Margaret Mussentine before John Hewter, Esq., justice of the peace of the Philadelphia Co., Pa., district of Southwark. She says that about Apr. of 1802 John Crawford calling himself Robinson came to her house on Plumb Street in Southwark and took lodging for himself and his wife. They stayed there three days and three nights and one morning she saw them in bed together. Margaret Mussentine signed her deposition "by mark."

Jan. 1, 1803 - Israel Israel, sheriff of Philadelphia Co. and City testified that on Dec. 15, 1802, he had William Hartung serve the subpoena on John Crawford to appear in court to answer the libel of his wife, Ann Crawford, for a divorce.

Sept. 18, 1802 - The Supreme Court of Pennsylvania, issued a subpoena to Francis Gallacher to appear before the Supreme Court of Pennsylvania, at Philadelphia, Pa., on the first Monday of Dec. 1802 to answer the libel of his wife Leah Gallacher for a divorce.

Oct. 1, 1802 - Petition of Leah Gallacher, wife of Francis Gallacher, late of the borough of Lancaster, schoolmaster, by her next friend William Armstrong. They were married about eleven years ago. Leah lived with her husband until March 9 or 10 of 1802. She considered him "naturally impotent and incapable of procreation from the time of their intermarriage and that he still continues to be so."

Dec. 1802 - Michael Rine, sheriff of Lancaster Co., Pa., testified that Francis Gallacher was not in his bailiwick and a copy of the subpoena was left at his last place of residence.

Jan. 1, 1803 - The Supreme Court of Pennsylvania, appointed John Oliver, Esq., associate judge of Mifflin Co., Pa., to be a Commissioner in this case.

Jan. 1, 1803 - The Supreme Court of Pennsylvania, issued a subpoena to Francis Gallacher to appear before the Supreme Court of Pennsylvania, in Philadelphia, Pa., on the first Monday of Mar. in 1803 to answer the libel of his wife, Leah Gallacher for a divorce.

Mar. 29, 1803 - Deposition of George Bratton before John Oliver, associate judge of Mifflin Co., Pa. He knew both parties in this case more than ten years. They lived together as man and wife until the beginning of 1802 for nine years but had no children. He testified that he had felt the private parts of Francis Gallacher and verily believes him to be without testicles.

Mar. 9, 1804 - Letter by Mr. T. Hopkins, counsel for libelant to Francis Gallacher to appear before the Supreme Court of Pennsylvania, at Philadelphia, Pa., on Mar. 21, 1804, to disprove his wife's allegation that he is impotent due to the absence of testicles.

Jan. 1, 1803 - The Supreme Court of Pennsylvania, issued a subpoena to William Thompson to appear before the Supreme Court of Pennsylvania, in Philadelphia, Pa., Mar. 26, 1803, to answer the libel of his wife, Jane Thompson, for a divorce.

Jan. 24, 1803 - Petition of Jane Thompson by George McDill, her next friend. She lives in Salsbury Twp., Lancaster Co., Pa., and was married nine years ago to William Thompson. He removed her to the western territory and there banished her from his bed and board and took up with another woman with whom he cohabited. She went to Kentucky where she had some friends. "He then followed me and wished to put me to sale which frightened me very much and obliged me to leave that state and come to Lancaster County to my father's."

Mar. 24, 1803 - Thomas Martin of Shippensburg, Cumberland Co., Pa., testified that he served the subpoena on William Thompson "at Miles settlement near Little Frence Creek either in County of Crawford or Erie, deponent doesn't perfectly know which." He read the subpoena and left a copy with William Thompson Mar. 9, 1803. "William Thompson is now resident in that settlement." Testified before Adam Reigart, justice of the peace in Lancaster Co., Pa.

Mar. 26, 1803 - The Supreme Court of Pennsylvania, issued a subpoena to William Thompson to appear before the Supreme Court of Pennsylvania, in Philadelphia, Pa., on the first Monday of Sept.

1803 to answer the libel of his wife, Jane Thompson, for a divorce.

Mar. 27, 1803 - The Supreme Court of Pennsylvania, appointed Thomas Foster and William Wallace of Erie Co., Pa., to take deposition in this case.

Aug. 24, 1803 - Deposition at the house of Thomas Foster, Esq. in the town of Erie, Pa., of William Cochran of Union Twp., Erie Co., Pa., yeoman, aged 36 years. William Cochran testified that he never saw Jane Thompson but is well acquainted with William Thompson who now resides in Union Twp. with a woman formerly called Sarah Tuttle now Sarah W. Henry. He has lived near William Thompson about four years. Sarah lived with William Thompson on and off during that time and she has two children, one "upwards of three years old" and the other about seventeen or eighteen months old. "The general opinion of the neighborhood is that Defendant is the father of the said children."

Aug. 24, 1803 - Deposition of Samuel Hutchin of Union Twp., Erie Co., Pa., farmer, aged nineteen years. He was well acquainted with William Thompson but had never seen Jane Thompson. William Thompson lived near him over three years with a woman formerly called Sarah Tuttle now called Sarah W. Henry. She lived with him most of this time and she has two children "of whom Defendant is reputed to be the father." Samuel Hutchin signed his deposition "by mark."

Aug. 24, 1803 - Deposition of Wheaton West of Waterford Twp., Erie Co., Pa., farmer, aged twenty-four years. He never saw Jane Thompson but was well acquainted with William Thompson. About three years ago Sarah Tuttle, now called Sarah W. Henry, was living with William Thompson and had lived with him for a year before that. She now has two children of which William Thompson is reputed to be the father. Wheaton West signed his deposition "by mark."

Aug. 24, 1803 - Deposition of John Willy of Waterford Twp., Erie Co., Pa., aged thirty-two years. He testified he only saw Jane Thompson once but was well acquainted with William Thompson. William Thompson lives in Union Twp., Erie Co., Pa., and "a woman formerly called Sarah Tuttle now Sarah W. Henry has resided with him generally from the month of Jan. or Feb. 1799 to the present time." He has known William Thompson as a near neighbor since the spring of 1797 and soon thereafter his wife Jane left him and never returned. Sarah Tuttle, now known as Sarah W. Henry, has two children, one aged about three years and one aged about eighteen months. The general opinion of the country is that William Thompson is their father.

Aug. 24, 1803 - Deposition of Wilson Smith of the Town of Waterford, Erie Co., Pa., innkeeper, aged thirty-two years. He never saw Jane Thompson but is well acquainted with William Thompson but never at his house. William Thompson lives in Union Twp., Erie Co.,

Pa. He has known William Thompson about four years. Sarah Tuttle, or Sarah W. Henry, has two children, one aged about three years and the other upwards of a year and William Thompson is reputed to be their father.

Aug. 24, 1803 - Deposition of James Anderson, Esq., of the Town of Erie, Erie Co., Pa., aged thirty-seven years. He never saw Jane Thompson but has been well acquainted with William Thompson from the summer of 1800 to the present time. William Thompson lives in Union Twp., Erie Co., Pa. In the summer of 1800, a certain Sarah Tuttle, since called Sarah W. Henry, lived with him. At that time she had a young child of which he was told William Thompson was the father. The house of William Thompson was small with but one bed.

Aug. 25, 1803 - Thomas Foster and William Wallace wrote the Supreme Court of Pennsylvania, that the service of witnesses could not be obtained without promise of compensation for their travel to Erie, Pa. They submitted a bill for William Cochran going and returning 54 miles; Samuel Hutchin going and returning 54 miles; Wheaton West going and returning 22 miles; John Willy going and returning 22 miles; and Wilson Smith going and returning 30 miles."

Sept. 3, 1803 - Thomas Martin testified before William Bausman, justice of the peace in Lancaster Co., Pa., that he served the subpoena on William Thompson by leaving him a copy Aug. 15, 1803, at his house for him to appear before the Supreme Court of Pennsylvania, at Philadelphia to answer the libel of his wife, Jane Thompson, for a divorce.

Sept. 17, 1802 - The Supreme Court of Pennsylvania, issued a subpoena to Charles Keef to appear before the Supreme Court of Pennsylvania, on Dec. 31, 1802, to answer the libel of his wife, Ann Keef, for a divorce.

Feb. 19, 1803 - Petition of Ann Keef by her next friend, John Young, was sworn before William Steele, justice of the peace in Lancaster Co., Pa. About two years and ten months age Ann had married Charles Keef. About four months later he deserted her and lived in a state of adultery with a married woman, Elizabeth O'Hogan.

Mar. 21, 1803 - The Supreme Court of Pennsylvania, issued a subpoena to Charles Keef to appear before the Supreme Court of Pennsylvania, in Philadelphia, Pa., on the first Monday of Sept. 1803 to answer the libel of his wife, Ann Keef, for a divorce.

Aug. 2, 1803 - Michael Rine, sheriff of Lancaster Co., Pa., testified he could not find Charles Keef in his bailiwick but left a copy of the subpoena Jul. 11, 1803, at the house of George Rahm in Rapho Twp., Lancaster Co., Pa., the last place of abode for Charles Keef. His bill was for twelve miles travel to serve this subpoena.

Dec. 3, 1803 - John Reitzel, sheriff of Lancaster Co., Pa., testified that Charles Keef was not in his bailiwick and he left a copy of the subpoena for Charles Keef on Dec. 2, 1802, at the house of John Hipple in Rapho Twp., Lancaster Co., Pa., the last abode of Charles Keef. He also caused proclamation in the Lancaster Co., Pa., Courthouse on three days for the appearance of Charles Keef.

Dec. 27, 1803 - Deposition of Robert Miller of Manheim Twp., Lancaster Co., Pa., who was concietiously [sic] scrupulous of taking an Oath. He had known Ann and Charles Keef nearly four years which was previous to their marriage. He knows they married in the spring or summer of 1800 and believes they lived as man and wife about four months. He heard a conversation between them in which plaintiff alleged defendant had beat her but defendant denied it. Charles Keef left his wife about four months after their marriage and sometime afterward he had a conversation with Robert Miller. Charles Keef told him that he had formed an intimacy with the wife of Thomas O'Hogan in Manheim Twp., Lancaster Co., Pa. They met one evening at the Glass House in Manheim Twp. and he repeatedly had carnal knowledge of her. He intended to go to Philadelphia and take Mrs. O'Hogan with him. He tried to persuade Charles Keef not to do this without any success on two occasions. Charles Keef did indeed leave and Mrs. O'Hogan went with him. Neither has returned to their marriage mates.

Dec. 27, 1803 - Deposition of John Arndt. He was not acquainted with Ann Keef but had often seen Charles Keef in Manheim Twp. but had no particular acquaintance with him. He had often heard that Charles Keef had left his wife. One morning about three years ago he set out from Manheim for Philadelphia. He met up with Charles Keef and Mrs. O'Hogan on the road about seven miles from Manheim. "They both endeavored to conceal themselves from this affirmant, she threw her cloak over her fact. This affirmant did not speak to them. Thomas O'Hogan's wife has not returned to Manheim or to her husband."

Dec. 27, 1803 - Deposition of Thomas O'Hogan who was not acquainted with Ann Keef but with Charles Keef. After Charles Keef came to Manheim it was generally said he was a married man. He had married Ann Liggett in Colrain Twp., Lancaster Co., Pa., in the fall of 1790. Thomas O'Hogan said he went to Huntington, Pa., to look for a place for his family to live. He wrote for his wife to come with his family. George Henberger was about to move from Manheim to that neighborhood also so he engaged George Henberger to take his wife and furniture in his waggons [sic]. About two months later he received word that his wife had sent off with Charles Keef. She never returned and he doesn't know where she is. They have been married about six years.

Dec. 27, 1803 - Deposition of Mary Liggett, sister of Ann Keef. She knew her sister Ann married Charles Keef in Apr. of 1800 as she was present at the wedding. They lived together about four months.

Charles Keef beat Ann several times severely. "The last beating that he gave her her breast was black for the space of six weeks. He beat her for coming to see her mother who was then very ill and not expected to live."

Dec. 31, 1803 - John Barker, sheriff of Philadelphia Co., Pa., testified that he made public declaration several market days and in public newspapers for four successive weeks for the appearance of Charles Keef in court to answer the libel of his wife for a divorce.

Feb. 26, 1803 - Petition of Mary Hackleroth of Warwick Twp., Lancaster Co., Pa., by her next friend, John Smith. She had married in Apr. of 1796 John Hackleroth and about five years ago he deserted her without any just cause. He also frequently beat her severely and treated her cruelly. One time he attempted to shoot her and another time he stabbed her with a large knife. Mary Hackleroth signed her petition in German script.

Mar. 26, 1803 - The Supreme Court of Pennsylvania, issued a subpoena to John Hackleroth to appear before the Supreme Court of Pennsylvania, in Philadelphia, Pa., on the first Monday of Sept. 1803 to answer the libel of his wife, Mary Hackleroth, for a divorce.

Aug. 2, 1803 - Michael Rine, sheriff of Lancaster Co., Pa., said he could not find John Hackleroth in his bailiwick and left a copy of the subpoena at the home of John Guyor in Warwick Twp., Lancaster Co., Pa., Jul. 11, 1803. He traveled ten miles to serve the subpoena.

Sept. 17, 1803 - The Supreme Court of Pennsylvania, issued a subpoena to John Hackleroth to appear before the Supreme Court of Pennsylvania, in Philadelphia, Pa., Dec. 31, 1803, to answer the libel of his wife, Mary Hackleroth, for a divorce.

Dec. 3, 1803 - John Reitzel, sheriff of Lancaster Co., Pa., testified John Hackleroth was not in his bailiwick. On Dec. 2, 1803, he had left a copy of the subpoena at the home of John Guyor in Warwick Twp., Lancaster Co., Pa., the place of his last residence. He also had caused proclamation for his appearance in court at the Lancaster Co., Pa., courthouse on three different days. John Baker, sheriff of the City and Co. of Philadelphia, also testified he had made public proclamation at the courthouse on three different days and made public notice in local newspapers for four successive weeks for the appearance of John Hackleroth to answer the libel of his wife, Mary Hackleroth, for a divorce.

Dec. 5, 1803 - The Supreme Court of Pennsylvania, appointed Paul Zantzinger and Adam Reigart, Jr. to be commissioners in this case.

Dec. 27, 1803 - Deposition of Henry Foltz who knew that John Hackleroth and Mary Hackleroth were married about seven years and nine months ago and they lived together for two years. About five years and nine months ago, John Hackleroth left his wife and never returned. He was present when John Hackleroth scolded and abused his wife very much. "He was a very ill-tempered man and always considered in the neighborhood as a very worthless character. Defendant once came to affirmant's with a gun and said he was in search of Plaintiff's father and if he could find him he would shoot him. Plaintiff always supported a good character and was much respected by her neighbors."

Dec. 27, 1803 - Deposition of John Freymer who was present at the wedding of John and Mary Hackleroth about seven years and nine months ago. They lived together about two years. John Hackleroth left his wife and never returned. The day he left, he was present and saw John Hackleroth with a gun in his hand threaten to shoot his wife. "He pushed her over an iron pot and was near puting her in the fire. She gave him no provocation whatsoever. He was always considered a man of very bad disposition and of bad character. Plaintiff always supported a good character and was much respected in her neighborhood."

Dec. 27, 1803 - Deposition of George Grier. Plaintiff was his daughter. She was married to John Hackleroth about seven years and nine months ago and they lived in his house together about three months thereafter. He treated her "very ill" during that time and often abused her without any cause. He would often get out of bed and go away all night. They then went to live in a house he owned about a fourth of a mile from his own. Frequently his daughter would come to his house crying and complaining of her husband's abuse.

Mar. 26, 1803 - The Supreme Court of Pennsylvania, issued a subpoena to John Oderwald to appear before the Supreme Court of Pennsylvania, in Philadelphia, Pa., Sept. 17, 1803, to answer the libel of his wife, Hannah Oderwald, for a divorce.

Jun. 27, 1803 - Petition of Hannah Oderwald by her next friend Peter Weily. She married John Oderwald in the borough of Lancaster, Pa., by Rev. Muhlenberg some years ago. Some months later he deserted her without any just cause or reason. She doesn't know where he now resides. Both Hannah Oderwald and Peter Weiley signed this petition "by mark."

Sept. 17, 1803 - The Supreme Court of Pennsylvania, appointed William Bausman, Esq., and John Light, Esq., to be commissioners to take depositions in this case.

Sept. 17, 1803 - The Supreme Court of Pennsylvania, issued a subpoena to John Oderwald to appear before the Supreme Court of Pennsylvania, in Philadelphia, Pa., on Dec. 31, 1803, to answer the libel of his wife, Hannah Oderwald, for a divorce.

Nov. 11, 1803 - Daniel Haines, constable in the borough of Lancaster, testified that he could not find John Oderwald in Lancaster Borough or Lancaster Co.. He left a copy of the subpoena at the house of George Fisher, innkeeper in the borough of Lancaster,

Pa., the last place of residence. At the time John Oderwald left the house was occupied "by one Kohl - a new house having been since erected on said lot of ground."

Dec. 20, 1803 - Deposition of Hanna Barter of Graff's Town, Lancaster Co., Pa. The libellant is her daughter. Over five years ago she married John Ordwald. She was present when the Rev. Henry Muhlenberg married them. Four years ago last spring John Orderwald deserted his wife - on or about Apr. 29, 1799. Her daughter, Hannah Oderwald, now lives with her at her house and occasionally hires out and has no other means of support. She didn't know where John Oderwald went. Hanna Barter signed her deposition "by mark."

Dec. 31, 1803 - John Reitzel, sheriff of Lancaster Co., Pa., reported that John Oderwald was not to be found in his bailiwick and that he had made public proclamation in the courthouse on three days (the 16, 17, and 18 of month). John Barker, sheriff of the city and county of Philadelphia, testified he made public proclamation on three days at the courthouse and in the Philadelphia, Pa., newspaper for four successive weeks for the appearance in court of John Oderwald to answer the libel of his wife, Hannah Oderwalt, for a divorce.

Dec. 31, 1803 - The Supreme Court of Pennsylvania, granted Hannah Oderwald a divorce from her husband, John Oderwalt.

Sept. 17, 1803 - The Supreme Court of Pennsylvania, issued a subpoena to Francis Fordney to appear before the Supreme Court of Pennsylvania, at Philadelphia, Pa., Dec. 31, 1803, to answer the libel of his wife, Elizabeth Fordney, for a divorce.

Nov. 28, 1803 - Petition of Elizabeth Fordney by her next friend Matthias Young. She was married about twenty-seven years ago to Francis Fordney then of the borough of Lancaster, Pa. Without any just or reasonable cause he deserted her for four or five years. He then returned and lived with her for one year and then deserted her again. They have been separated upwards of eighteen years. Elizabeth Fordney signed her petition "by mark."

Dec. 5, 1803 - The Supreme Court of Pennsylvania, issued a subpoena to Francis Fordney to appear before the Supreme Court of Pennsylvania, on the second Monday of Mar. 1804 to answer the libel of his wife, Elizabeth Fordney, for a divorce. John Reitzel, sheriff of Lancaster Co., Pa., testified that Francis Fordney was not to be found in his bailiwick and he made the proper declarations at the courthouse. John Barker, sheriff of the city and county of Philadelphia testified that he made three days proclamation on market days and gave the proper notice in public newspapers for the appearance in court of Francis Fordney to answer the libel of his wife, Elizabeth Fordney, for a divorce.

Dec. 19, 1803 - Daniel Kaines of the borough of Lancaster, Pa., testified before William Bausman, justice of the peace, that he left a copy of the subpoena at the house of Solomon Kauffman on King Street in Lancaster, Pa., being the place of last residence of Francis Fordney on Dec. 12, 1803, and was informed he was long absent and they had no knowledge of where he now is.

Dec. 31, 1803 - The Supreme Court of Pennsylvania, appointed William Beausman and John Light to be commissioners in this case and to take depositions in this case.

Feb. 6, 1804 - Letter from C. Smith, attorney for libellant to Edward Shippen Burd, Esq. asking if the sheriff had inserted his advertisments in the case of Elizabeth Fordney by her next friend, Matthias Young, vs. Francis Fordney as it would have to be done immediately. The commissioners are William Bausman and John Light.

Feb. 22, 1804 - Deposition of Peter Miller of the borough of Lancaster. He had known the Fordneys upwards of thirty years and before their marriage which took place before the Revolutionary War. About two years after their marriage they moved to McCallister's Town but returned later to Lancaster. Shortly thereafter, Francis Fordney left his wife and sometime later returned. Then about twenty years ago Francis Fordney again left his wife but never returned to Lancaster. He left debts behind him and no means of support for his wife. He dosen't known where Francis Fordney now is but his wife has always remained in Lancaster and has a respectable character.

Feb. 2, 1804 - Deposition of John Brenniman. He knew Francis Fordney left Lancaster, Pa., about twenty years ago owing much money. He also testified that he didn't know where Francis Fordney went but his wife remained in Lancaster, Pa., and has supported herself.

Mar. 21, 1804 - The Supreme Court of Pennsylvania, granted Elizabeth Fordney a divorce from Francis Fordney.

Lancaster Co., Pa., Appearance Docket May Term 1806 #26 - Margaret McFaddien [sic] by her next friend, James (Foley? Faley?), vs. Thomas McFaddien [sic], libel in divorce. Her petition stated that she married Thomas McFaddin (sic) May 22, 1792, and she left him on Dec. 10, 1805. On many occasions he "beat, bruised and otherwise ill-treated her." The petition was dated Feb. 11, 1806, and she signed "by mark."

Feb. 12, 1806 - Subpoena was issued to Thomas McFaddien to answer the libel of his wife, Margaret McFaddien, for a divorce.

Lancaster Co., Pa., Appearance Docket Aug. Term 1806 #104 - Mary McFaddian [sic] by her next friend James Falay vs. Thomas McFaddian [sic], libel in divorce. Original documents missing.

Lancaster Co., Pa., Appearance Docket May Term 1806 #27 - William Martin vs. Elizabeth Martin, libel in divorce.

Jan. 24, 1806 - Petition of William Martin of Earl Twp., Lancaster Co., Pa., who had married his present wife Elizabeth. She left him and married Akins Baxter and had two children by him. Subpoena issued May 15, 1806. Sheriff reported he could not find Elizabeth Martin but left the subpoena at her last place of abode in Cumberland Co., Pa.

Lancaster Co., Pa., Appearance Docket Aug. Term 1806 #38 - William Martin vs. Elizabeth Martin. Alias subpoena for libel in divorce issued Jan. 23, 1807. On Aug. 29, 1806, the court appointed Paul Zantzinger, Esq., to take depositions in this case.

Jan. 7, 1807 - Deposition of James Galt, justice of the peace of Earl Twp., Lancaster Co., Pa., who testified that Elizabeth Martin, wife of William Martin, left her husband in Dec. of 1799. She remained in the neighborhood awhile and then towards spring moved to Chambersburg, Franklin Co., Pa., and then married Aiken Baxter, son of John Baxter. She afterwards lived with one John Black one year and again with Lewis Heck until she had two children and afterwards lived with said Aiken Baxter and then moved with said "Aiken Baxter and his father John Baxter into the western world and has not been heard of since." On Jan. 23, 1807, the court granted William Martin a divorce from his wife, Elizabeth Martin.

Lancaster Co., Pa., Appearance Docket Aug. Term 1806 #39 - Elizabeth Harman by her next friend, George Arndt, vs. Conrad Harman - original documents missing.

Lancaster Co., Pa., Appearance Docket Aug. Term 1806 #40 - Dorethea Brendle vs. Philip Brendle, libel in divorce. Subpoena issued Jan. 23, 1807. Original documents missing.

Lancaster Co., Pa., Appearance Docket Aug. Term 1806 #41 - Rachel Miles by her next friend, George Adams, vs. James Miles, libel in divorce. Original documents missing.

Lancaster Co., Pa., Appearance Docket Nov. Term 1806 #48 - Rachel Miles by her next friend, George Adams, vs. James Miles, libel in divorce. On Jan. 23, 1807, the court appointed Paul Zantzenger, Esq., to take depositions in this case. Original documents missing.

Lancaster Co., Pa., Appearance Docket Nov. Term 1806 #144 - Hester Bader by her next friend, John Wilson, vs. Samuel Russell Bader, libel in divorce.

Nov. 17, 1806 - Petition of Hester Bader by her next friend, John Wilson, that she married Samuel Russell Bader on Oct. 15, 1794.

He deserted her Oct. 1, 1802. Subpoena to be left at home of Nathan Milners on the west branch of Octoraro in Colrain Twp.

Nov. 29, 1806 - Subpoena issued for Jan. Term 1807 and "Sheriff Emanuel Reigart reports he left it at the house of Nathan Milnor in Colerain Township, it being the usual and last abode of the said Samuel Russell Bader within my bailiwick." Alias subpoena issued Jan. 13, 1807. Court ordered that depositions in this case were to be taken before David Montgomery, Esq., on Apr. 23, 1807.

Apr. 4, 1807 - Deposition of Cyrus Milnor stating "the affirmant further sayeth that my father received a letter from Samuel Russell Bader praying him to send to Alexandria for the said Samuel and Hester his wife. I drove my father's team to Alexandria in the State of Virginia and loaded what property the said Samuel and said Hester wished to bring with them expecting the said Samuel would come along with his wife to my fathers in Colerain Township, Lancaster County. The said Samuel came a small distance and then told the affirmant that he could not go any further that he had some business to settle in the neighborhood of Alexandria but would come on to my fathers in four weeks from that time. That was in the month of November 1802. The said Samuel never came but separated himself from the said Hester from that time to the present day. The affirmant further sayeth that the said Samuel did not assist nor support the said Hester never since the separation."

Apr. 4, 1807 - Deposition of Mary Milnor that Samuel and Hester Bader left our house on Dec. 14, 1794, in company with Catharine Milnor to go to Chester. Catharine came home the next day and informed her that Samuel and Hester were married by a justice of the peace in Chester. "In the spring of 1795 I went to the City of Philadelphia to see the said Samuel and Hester his wife. I tarried there about one week. The said Samuel's conduct at that time appeared to be very cool and indifferant [sic] towards his wife. He appeared never to be in her company only at meal time and was out at night to a very late hour sometimes 10 and sometimes 11 o'clock. The day I left Philadelphia the said Samuel was missing and could not be found in the City. I came home and in a short time after the said Hester came to our house and said the said Samuel had not returned and we did not hear of the said Samuel for ten months after he left the City. We heard he was in the State of Virginia. The said Hester went after him and found him and resided with him till February 1798 at that time she came home almost naked and stayed some time and returned to him again to Virginia and lived with him till the last separation in November 1802."

Apr. 4, 1807 - Deposition of Leatitia Patter who testified that Hester Bader came to Nathan Kubnor's in Nov. of 1802 and lived principally there until this present time. "The said Hester has been prudent and industrious and respected by all the neighbors and acquantances [sic]."

Apr. 4, 1807 - Deposition of Catharine Wilson who was present at the marriage of Samuel and Hester Bader Dec. 14, 1794. He left her about two hours after they were married. "In 1798 the said Hester came to her fathers in Colerain Township, Lancaster Co. it being in the month of February with a young child both partly naked at that cold season. She then lived with her father about eighteen months and in the autumn of 1800 the affirmant sayeth that John Wilson, the affirmant's husband, took the said Hester Bader to her husband Samuel Russell Bader in the State of Virginia. The affirmant further sayeth that in the spring of 1802 Samuel Bader told Nathaniel Milnor, the father of the said Hester, that he wished him to build a house for him. The said Samuel to live in which I believe her father agreed to do. In the month of September 1802 the said Samuel wrote to the said Nathaniel Milnor, father-in-law to the said Samuel, to send for the said Samuel and his wife to Alexandria at the request of the said Samuel. The said Nathan [sic] sent his team to Alexandria for the said Samuel and the said Hester his wife. The said Hester arrived at said Nathan Milnors in November 1802 but the said Samuel did not come with the said Hester his wife."

On Apr. 23, 1807, the sheriff reported that he left the required subpoena at the house of Nathan Melnor where Samuel Russell Bader once lived. On Apr. 23, 1807, the court granted Hester Bader a divorce from her husband, Samuel Russell Bader.

Lancaster Co., Pa., Appearance Docket Jan. 1807 Term #76 - Catharine Burgart vs. George Burgart, libel in divorce.

Dec. 9, 1806 - Petition of Catharine Burgart who said she married George Burgart over twenty years ago. Over four years ago he left without any provision for her or her children.

Jan. 21, 1807 - The court issued a subpoeona to George Burgart to appear in court to answer the libel of his wife for a divorce. On Jan. 23, 1807, the court appointed Paul Zantzinger, Esq., to take depositions in this case.

Apr. 20, 1807 - Deposition of David Bear of Leacock Twp., Lancaster Co., Pa. He had known Caty Burkert [sic] several years. He heard that her husband visited her once but he never saw him. Catharine Burkert [sic] "hath been very industrious and struggled hard to maintain herself and children."

Apr. 24, 1807 - Deposition of Catherina Vonkenin, wife of Michael Vonkenin of Leacock Twp., Lancaster Co., Pa. Last Jan. four years ago, Catharine Burkhart [sic] wife of George Burkhart [sic] was brought to the house of Catharina Vonkenin, now deceased, by her brother Jacob Snebely with her only child a son about five or six years old. She was very sickly, in a poor state of health and in extreme poverty. Catharine lived with her about two years and during that time took in sewing, knitting and washed for neighbors, also baking cakes and brewing of beer. She went from there to the house of Abraham Johns, a friend. Another friend, Michael Hoss of Leacock Twp. helped her open a small store. In four years time, her husband never called to see her.

Apr. 24, 1807 - Deposition of Michael Hoss of Leacock Twp., Lancaster Co., Pa. He had known Catharine Burkhart since before her marriage. She lived with her brother, Jacob Snebely, in Cumberland Co., Pa. Then he brought her to the house of Catharine Vonkenin, now deceased, mother of Michael Vonkenin, in Jan. of 1802. Soon after her arrival he visited her and found her very sickly, broken-hearted and distressed. The prevailing report was that her husband had neglected her by gambling. She started taking in sewing, knitting and gaining strength went to her neighbors to take in wash. Later she started to bake cakes and brew beer. She took a house on the farm of Abraham Johns and opened a small store. Her husband came to her last winter but she turned him away and he has not been heard of since. He signed his name "Michael Hess."

Apr. 24, 1807 - Deposition of George Bender of Leacock Twp., Lancaster Co., Pa. Last fall five years ago he returned from Md., and visited his uncle, Jacob Snebely, who lived in Cumberland Co. about two miles from Harrisburg, Pa. Catharine Burkert was living with his uncle. She told him how she had walked there with her five children. She was very sickly and appeared in great distress and poverty. After her arrival at Catharine VonKenin's [sic] his father hearing of her distressed condition sent this despondant's brother John with two horses loaded with flour, meat and all kinds of vegetables for her support.

Apr. 27, 1807 - A subpoena was issued for George Burgart to appear in court to answer the libel of his wife, Catharine Burgart, for a divorce. The sheriff reported that he could not find him in his bailiwick.

Aug. 27, 1807 - An alias subpoena was again issued for George Burgart to appear in court to answer the libel of his wife, Catharine Burgart, for a divorce. Sheriff Emanuel Reigart reported that he could not find him in his bailiwick.

Oct. 9, 1807 - Deposition of Mary Ford, wife of John Ford of Harrisburg, Pa., that "in the fall of 1801 at the time the Indian corn was taken home that Caty Burkhart [sic] her aunt came to the house of her father's in the afternoon. As she came into the house with her two children, the latter barefooted, and all badly cloathed [sic]. From their appearance as they came into the house we the children said to each other there comes a baggar [sic] with her two children. When said Caty Burkhart [sic] accosted the children and said she supposed they did not know her and said I am Caty Burkhart [sic] your father's sister - upon which we all ran out to call our father and informed him that their aunt had arrived with her two children, upon which he came into the house and appeared much agitated and felt much for her, and gave her a hearty wellcome [sic] and during her stay with him he did everything to comfort her, feed and clothed the children and found her in boarding and cloathing [sic] as one of his own family, during upwards of a year, and untill [sic] this Deponant's [sic] father married (who was a widower) she and her children lived in the family. That during all this time her husband never made his appearance in the family nor did we know what became of him - and that her aunt to her knowledge heard of him nor got the least support from him. After the marriage of this Deponant's [sic] father her aunt then left them, and was conveyed by her father together with her children to widow VonKenen [sic] their grandmother. That during her aunt's stay in our family she was allmost [sic] constantly very poorly and often very sick." Mary Ford signed her depostion "by mark."

Nov. 21, 1807, the court granted Catharine Burgart a divorce from her husband, George Burgart.

Lancaster Co., Pa., Appearance Docket Jan. Term 1807 #77 - John Henry vs. Bridget Henry, libel in divorce.

Jan. 26, 1807 - Petition of John Henry of the borough of Lancaster, Pa., that he married his present wife, Bridget Henry, Apr. 6, 1806. He accused her of adultery. Subpoena issued for Aug. Term 1807. Alias subpoena issued for Nov. Term 1807. Undated deposition of James Archer of the borough of Lancaster, Pa., nailer. He knew the plaintiff and defendant since Oct. 31, 1806, as he boarded and slept in their home. He accused Bridget Henry of drinking and adultery and that she frequently accused her husband of adultery and threatened his life, etc. He never saw him strike her or treat her ill. James Archer signed his deposition "by mark." Court decreed that proclamation in this case be made Nov. 18, 20, and 21 of 1807.

Lancaster Co., Pa., Appearance Docket Apr. Term 1807 #95 - Doretha Brendle by her next friend John Snyder vs. Philip Brendle, libel in divorce. Court appointed Paul Zantzinger, Esq., to take depositions in this case on Apr. 23, 1807.

Apr. 27, 1807 - Deposition of John Kain who testified that Philip Brendle was a gambler, swindler, and a cheat. For at least a year Philip Brendle was in Harrisburg Goal [sic] for purgery. Upon release he went back to gambling, swindling, and cheating and he did not support his wife. Leaving Harrisburg, Pa., he went south and last he heard he was in the Baltimore, Md., Goal [sic]. He left his wife at least four years ago. On Apr. 27, 1807, the court decreed a divorce for Doretha Brendle from her husband, Philip Brendle.

Lancaster Co., Pa., Appearance Docket Jan. Term 1808 #89 - Catherine McCasland by her next friend, Jacob Baker, vs. Daniel McCasland, libel in divorce.

Dec. 26, 1807, petition of Catherine McCasland that she married

David McCasland in the autumn of 1803. Four years and upwards thereafter he deserted her without any just or reasonable cause. Jan. 21, 1808, the court issued a subpoena for Daniel McCasland to appear before the court Apr. Term 1808 to answer the libel of his wife, Catherine McCasland, for a divorce.

Alias subpoena issued Mar. 3, 1808, and Apr. 27, 1808, for Daniel McCasland to appear in court to answer the libel of his wife Catherine McCasland for a divorce. Apr. 27, 1808, the court appointed Martin Carpenter, Esq., to take depositions in this case. Also on Apr. 27, 1808, Sheriff Emanuel Reigart reported that he "served personaly [sic] on the body of the Defendant in this case and left a copy of this subpoena with him at least fifteen days before the Commencement of April Term 1808." He also stated that Daniel McCasland "lives at or near Major William McCasland."

Lancaster Co., Pa., Appearance Docket Jan. Term 1808 #90 - Catherine Hains by her next friend, Andrew Rudy, vs. Samuel Hains, libel in divorce.

Jan. 13, 1808 - Petition of Catharina Haines that she married Samuel Haines in 1784. He deserted her over two years ago without any just or reasonable cause. Catharine Haines signed her petition "by mark."

Jan. 21, 1808 - Court issued a subpoena to Samuel Haines to appear in court to answer the libel of his wife, Catharine Haines, for a divorce.

Nov. 4, 1808 - The court issued an alias subpoena to Samuel Haines to appear in court to answer the libel of his wife, Catharine Haines, for a divorce.

Nov. 4, 1808 - The court appointed Paul Zantinger, Esq. to take depositions in this case.

Jan. 26, 1809 - The court granted Catherine Haines a divorce from her husband, Samuel Hains.

Lancaster Co., Pa., Appearance Docket Jan. Term 1809 #65 - John Hartman vs. Elizabeth Hartman, libel in divorce.

Jan. 21, 1809 - Petition of John Hartman of Manor Twp., Lancaster Co., Pa., He married Feb. 22, 1801, Elizabeth, the daughter of Jacob Brua. His wife was convicted of adultery by the Jan. Term 1809 Court of Quarter Sessions, copy enclosed. She was convicted of adultery with Philip Kehler by which she had twin bastard children, a boy and a girl. She was sentenced to three months in Lancaster County Jail, to pay the costs of prosecution and to pay a fine of $5.00 to the commonwealth of Pa.

Jan. 28, 1809 - The court issued a subpoena to Elizabeth Hartman to appear in court to answer the libel of her husband, John Hartman, for a divorce.

Jan. 28, 1809 - The sheriff reported he served Elizabeth Hartman with the subpoena.

Apr. 29, 1809 - The court issued an alias subpoena for Elizabeth Hartman to appear in court to answer the libel of her husband, John Hartman, for a divorce.

Apr. 29, 1809 - Sheriff reported that he had served the alias subpoena on Elizabeth Hartman.

Aug. 26, 1809 - The court granted John Hartman a divorce from his wife Elizabeth Hartman.

Lancaster Co., Pa., Appearance Docket Aug. Term 1809 #175 - George Eicholtz vs. Mary Eicholtz, libel in divorce. Petition for a divorce filed.

Aug. 21, 1809 - The court issued a subpoena for Mary Eicholtz to appear in court on the third Monday of Nov. 1809 to answer the libel of her husband, George Eicholtz, for a divorce.

Aug. 28, 1809 - The court issued an alias subpoena for the Jan. Term 1810 for Mary Eicholtz to appear in court to answer the libel of her husband, George Eicholtz, for a divorce.

Jan. 15, 1810 - The court appointed Paul Zantzing, Esq. to take depositions in this case.

Jan. 17, 1810 - The court granted George Eicholtz a divorce from his wife, Mary Eicholtz. Original papers are now missing.

Lancaster Co., Pa., Appearance Docket Aug. Term 1809 #176 - Elizabeth Bare vs. John Bare, petition for a divorce.

Aug. 25, 1809 - Elizabeth Bare petioned the court that she married John Bare in Feb. of 1804. He deserted her three months later without any just or reasonable cause. Elizabeth Bare signed her petition "by mark."

Aug. 25, 1809 - The court issued a subpoena for John Bare to appear in court on the third Monday of Nov. 1809 to answer the libel of his wife, Elizabeth Bare, for a divorce. The sheriff reported that the plaintiff was not to be found.

Lancaster Co., Pa., Appearance Docket Aug. Term 1809 #177 - Elizabeth Tillotson vs. Jeffery Tillotson, libel in divorce.

Aug. 21, 1809 - Petition of Elizabeth Tillotson by her next friend, John Martin, stated that she married Jeffery Tillotson Feb. 2, 1807. He deserted her Oct. 8, 1807, without any just or reasonable cause and "hath since that time lived in a constant practice of adultery with another woman." Her petition was read before the court Aug. 21, 1809, and that same day a subpoena was issued to Jeffery Tillotson to appear in court on the third Monday of Nov. 1809 to answer the libel of his wife for a divorce. Sheriff returned that he served this subpoena.

Jan. 23, 1810 - The court appointed Paul Zantzinger, Esq., to take depositions in this case.

Lancaster Co., Pa., Appearance Docket Jan. Term 1810 #91 - Ann Nichols by her uncle and next friend Samuel Funk vs. Austin Nichols, libel in divorce.

Jan. 17, 1810 - Petition of Ann Nichols stated that she married Austin Nichols Aug. 20, 1801, in Lancaster Co., Pa., where she was born and has always lived. They had three children. He abandoned her Jul. 4, 1805, without any just or reasonable cause leaving her and her three children destitute. She doesn't know where he has gone. She signed her petition "by mark."

Jan. 17, 1810 - The petition was read to the court and a subpoena was issued for Austin Nichols to appear in court on the third Monday of Apr. 1810 to answer the libel of his wife, Ann Nichols, for a divorce.

Apr. 19, 1810 - An alias subpoena was issued for Austin Nichols to appear in court to answer the libel of his wife, Ann Nichols, for a divorce.

Apr. 19, 1810 - The court appointed William Barton, Esq., to take depositions in this case.

Aug. 23, 1810 - The court granted Ann Nichols a divorce from her husband, Austin Nichols.

Lancaster Co., Pa., Appearance Docket Apr. Term 1810 #64 - Ann Hammond by her next friend, William Barclay, vs. Thomas Hammond, libel in divorce.

Jan. 27, 1810 - Petition of Ann Hammond by her next friend William Barclay stated that she married in Nov. of 1804 Thomas Hammond "without the knowledge or consent of her parents, being then young and unexperienced." Thomas Hammond was cruel and harsh to his wife and he left her in Jun. of 1805 without any just or reasonable cause.

Jan. 27, 1810 - Court issued a subpoena for Thomas Hammond to appear in court to answer the libel of his wife, Ann Hammond, for a divorce.

Apr. 18, 1810 - Court issued an alias subpoena for Thomas Hammond to appear in court to answer the libel of his wife, Ann Hammond, for a divorce.

Apr. 18, 1810 - Court appointed David Montgomery, Esq., to take depositions in this case.

Lancaster Co., Pa., Appearance Docket Aug. Term 1810 #34 - Ann Hammond by her next friend, William Barclay, vs. Thomas Hammond.

Aug. 21, 1810 - Court appointed Paul Zantzinger, Esq., to take depositions.

Aug. 22, 1810 - Court granted Ann Hammond a divorce from her husband, Thomas Hammond. Original documents are now missing which apparently include the depositions gathered.

Lancaster Co., Pa., Appearance Docket Jan. Term 1811 #5 - Elizabeth Reihm by her next friend, Coleman H. Taylor, vs. Abraham Reihm, libel in divorce.

Jan. 22, 1811 - Court appointed John Light, Esq., to take depositions in this case.

Jan. 23, 1811 - Court granted Elizabeth Reihm a divorce from her husband, Abraham Reihm. Original documents are now missing which apparently include the depositions gathered.

Lancaster Co., Pa., Appearance Docket Jan. Term 1811 #41 - Elizabeth Rea by her next friend, Michael Withers, vs. James Rhea [sic], libel in divorce.

Jan. 23, 1811 - Court appointed George Matter, Esq., to take depositions in this case.

Jan. 25, 1811 - Court granted Elizabeth Rea [sic] a divorce from her husband, James Rhea [sic]. Original documents are now missing which apparently include the depositions gathered.

Lancaster Co., Pa., Appearance Docket Apr. Term 1811 #45-John Barr vs. Elizabeth Barr, libel in divorce.

Jan. 22, 1811 - Petition of John Barr who "married about seven years last past to a certain Elizabeth Clous of Donegal Township in the said county. That your petitioner cohabited with the said Elizabeth about four weeks, but finding that the said Elizabeth was pregnant, unknown to your petitioner, and whereby your petitioner was greatly distressed, your petitioner ceased to cohabit with her, nor has he ever since cohabited with her. That business calling your petitioner abroad into one of the western Counties of this State, he left the county early in the year 1805, and has never since seen the said Elizabeth. That the said Elizabeth has continued to live a lewd life and upwards of a year after your petitioner left home was delivered of a Bastard child, which your petitioner is fully able to prove and as he is informed and verily believes, she still continues in a state of lewdness."

Apr. 16, 1811 - Alias subpoena was issued for Elizabeth Barr to appear in court to answer the libel of her husband, John Barr, for a divorce.

Apr. 16, 1811 - Court appointed Alexander Boggs, Esq., of Donegal Twp. to examine witnesses in this case.

Lancaster Co., Pa., Appearance Docket Aug. Term 1811 #23 - John Barr vs. Elizabeth Barr, libel in divorce. Alias subpoena issued for Elizabeth Barr to appear in court to answer the libel of her husband, John Barr, for a divorce. Proclamations made on Aug. 19, 20, 21, and 24 of 1811.

Aug. 24, 1811 - Deposition of Christian Shelly of Mt. Joy Twp., Lancaster Co., Pa., "conscienciously scrupulous of taking an oath."

He declared he had known Elizabeth Barr since she was a child. She was the daughter of Adam Klaus. He knew she had a child last fall "while residing and cohabiting with Francis McGlauchlin, with whom she continues to reside and cohabit and that he was informed by the said McGlauchlin, that he and the said Elizabeth had lived together upwards of one year, to the best of his recollection and belief."

Aug. 24, 1811 - Deposition of Catharine Klapper before James Whitehill. She testified that she was present when Elizabeth Barr had a child in harvest time five years past at the house of Elizabeth Alberts. At that time John Barr had been absent about twenty-two months. She saw Elizabeth Barr "about two weeks ago who said she now had another child and that she was married to one McGlauchlin." Catharine Klapper signed her deposition "by mark."

Aug. 24, 1811 - Deposition of John Smith of Donegal Twp., Lancaster Co., Pa., before James Whitehill. He testified that he knew John Barr went to Somerset County, Pa., in Feb. of 1804 a few months after his marriage. He was gone between twenty months and twenty-four months. About fifteen months after he left, his wife had a child while she lived at the house of Elizabeth Alberts.

Aug. 24, 1811 - The court granted John Barr a divorce from his wife, Elizabeth Barr.

Lancaster Co., Pa., Appearance Docket Nov. Term 1811 #30 - Elizabeth Burke by her next friend, Philip Gloninger, vs. James Burke, libel in divorce.

Aug. 28, 1811 - Petition of Elizabeth Burke by her next friend Philip Gloninger that she married in Harford Co., Md., James Burke in Mar. of 1794. They moved from Harford Co., Md., to Conecocheagree, then to Md., then to Octoraro, then to the borough of Lancaster "each of which places he sucessively left to avoid paying the debts he contracted thro [sic] his profilgacy and idleness." He deserted her in Aug. of 1805 without any reasonable cause leaving his wife and four children "in the most distressing circumstances." He came back once to ask her "to go with him to the westward" but he never returned to live with her or give her and the children any support. "The said James Burk [sic] in further violation of his marriage vow in the year 1807 knowingly entered into a second marriage in the County of Lycoming and hath been guilty of other adulterous acts."

Aug. 28, 1811 - Court issued a subpoena to James Burke at the defendant's last place of abode for him to appear in court to answer the libel of his wife, Elizabeth Burke, for a divorce.

Nov. 19, 1811 - Court appointed William Bird Ross to take depositions in this case.

Lancaster Co., Pa., Appearance Docket Jan. Term 1812 #10 - Elizabeth Burk [sic] by her next friend, Philip Gloninger, vs. James Burk [sic], libel in divorce.

Apr. 11, 1809 - Deposition of William Green, Esq., justice of the peace in Lycoming Co., Pa., testified that in 1807 a James Burk [*sic*] married Catherine Martin of Lycoming Co., Pa.

Oct. 24, 1809 - Deposition of John Street, justice of the peace of Harford Co., Md., that Rogers Street and Margaret Tate testified to him they were present when James Burk [*sic*] married Elizabeth North in Mar. of 1794 by a Rev. John Davis, now deceased.

Nov. 21, 1811 - Court issued a subpoena to James Burk [*sic*] to appear in court on the third Monday of Jan. 1812 to answer the libel of his wife, Elizabeth Burk [*sic*], for a divorce. James Humes, sheriff, reported that James Burk [*sic*] was not found in his bailiwick and he stated that he put public notice of the alias subpoena in the *United States Gazette*, a Philadelphia, Pa., newspaper for four successive weeks prior to the third Monday of 1812.

Jan. 21, 1812 - Deposition of Col. John Peden of Lancaster Co., Pa., who testified that James Burk [*sic*] was employed by him several years ago. He went to the western country above five years ago considerably in debt to him and to the best of his knowledge has not been back to Lancaster Co., Pa.

Jan. 27, 1812 - Sheriff reported that proclamation were made Jan. 21, 24, and 25 of 1812 for the appearance of James Burk [*sic*] to answer the libel of his wife, Elizabeth Burk [*sic*], for a divorce.

Jan. 27, 1812 - On the basis of depositions of John Peden, Rogers Sheet, and Margaret Tate, the court granted Elizabeth Burk [*sic*] a divorce from her husband, James Burk [*sic*].

Lancaster Co., Pa., Appearance Docket Nov. Term 1812 #44 - Christian Stauffer vs. Hannah Stauffer, libel in divorce.

Sept. 28, 1812 - Petition of Christian Stauffer of the village of Manheim, Rapho Twp., Lancaster Co., Pa., that he married his present wife, Hannah, on May 8, 1804. She has been convicted of adultery with Christian Nauman. On the third Monday of Aug. 1812, the court of Oyer and Terminer of Lancaster Co., Pa., met and it was shown that Hannah Stauffer committed adultery on Apr. 1, 1800, and at divers other times, up to the taking of this indictment. She pleaded not guilty but trial by jury declared her guilty. She was sentenced to pay five dollars fine to the Commonwealth and to serve three months servitute [*sic*] at the Public School of Lancaster Co., Pa., and to pay the costs of her prosecution. This sentence was dated Aug. 18, 1812. Divorce action was continued to Jan. Term 1813 #17.

Lancaster Co., Pa., Appearance Docket Jan. Term 1813 #17 - Christian Stauffer vs. Hannah Stauffer, libel in divorce. Original action was Nov. Term 1812 #44 and case was continued to Jan. Term 1815. Proclamation was made Jan. 17, 18, and 19 of 1815.

Jan. 19, 1815 - A certified copy of the Indictment and Conviction of Defendant for Adultery by said court was read and the court granted Christian Stauffer a divorce from his wife, Hannah Stauffer. Original documents for this case are now missing.

Lancaster Co., Pa., Appearance Docket Apr. Term 1813 #51 - Elizabeth Miller by her next friend, Peter Eby, vs. Michael Miller, libel in divorce.

Feb. 26, 1813 - Petition of Elizabeth Miller by her next friend Peter Eby that she was born in Pa., and now is nearly forty-five years of age and has always lived in Pa., and for the last ten years in Lancaster Co., Pa. She married Michael Miller about thirty years ago. Michael Miller deserted her about ten years ago without any just or reasonable cause with ten children and the youngest not more than nine days old. She has been informed that he now lives at or near Niagara. Elizabeth Miller signed her petition "by mark."

Mar. 5, 1813 - The court issued a subpoena to Michael Miller to appear in court to answer the libel of his wife, Elizabeth Miller, for a divorce.

Apr. 20, 1813 - Proclamations were made for Michael Miller to appear in court to answer the libel of his wife, Elizabeth Miller, for a divorce.

Apr. 22, 1813 - Alias subpoena was issued for the Aug. Term of 1813 for Michael Miller to appear in court at that time to answer the libel of his wife, Elizabeth Miller, for a divorce.

Apr. 22, 1813 - Court appointed Casper Shaffner and John Hoff, Esq., to take depositions in this case.

Lancaster Co., Pa., Appearance Docket Aug. Term 1813 #82 - Elizabeth Miller by her next friend, Peter Eby, vs. Michael Miller, libel in a divorce.

Apr. 22, 1813 - Court appointed Casper Shaffner and John Hoff to take depositions in this case.

May 6, 13, 20, and 27 of 1812 - Proclamation made in the *Lancaster Journal* for Michael Miller to appear in court to answer the libel of his wife, Elizabeth Miller, for a divorce.

Jun. 9, 1813 - Court issued an alias subpoena to Michael Miller to appear in court to answer the libel of his wife, Elizabeth Miller, for a divorce. Sheriff reported he served this alias subpoena by leaving it at the last place of residence in Lancaster Co., Pa., at George Britz's house and it took eleven miles to do this.

Jul. 10, 1813 - Deposition of Emanuel Dyer of the village of Manheim in Rapho Twp., Lancaster Co., Pa., before Casper Shaffner and John Hoff. He testified that he had known Michael Miller upwards of thirty years. About twenty-nine or thirty years ago Michael Miller married Elizabeth at the village of Manheim by William Smith, justice of the peace. Elizabeth Miller was the daughter of Abraham Huber. Michael Miller was a storekeeper in the village. The marriage "was a clandestine one, as the Deponant believes, not known at the time to the said Abraham" (bride's father). They lived in the village several years and had one child together. Then they moved to Campbell'stown, Dauphin Co., Pa., about ten years ago when he last talked to Michael Miller they were living at Campbell's-town. A few days later he heard "that Michael was missing and much search was made for him on a supposition that some accident had befallen him, but could not be found. Last he heard Michael was living at Niagara but he didn't know if that was true. He did understand that Michael and his wife lived disagreeably with each other." His observations were that Elizabeth Miller was a good, affectionate and faithful wife.

Aug. 23, 1813 - Deposition of Emanuel Dyer was read to the court and the court granted Elizabeth Miller a divorce from her husband, Michael Miller.

Lancaster Co., Pa., Appearance Docket Apr. Term 1813 #53 - Magdalena Elleberger by her next friend, Abraham Herr, vs. Ulrich Elleberger, libel in divorce.

Jan. 22, 1813 - Petition of Magdalene [sic] Elleberger, the wife of Ulrich Elleberger, of Manor Twp., Lancaster Co., Pa., laborer, by her next friend, Abraham Herr. "That about fifteen years ago your peti-tioner was intermarried with the said Ulrich Elleberger and has now five children. That during a period of nine years the said Ulrich has treated your petitioner in a cruel and barbarous manner. That within the last two years the said Ulrich has by his extreme barbari-ty and cruelty endangered her life and offered such indignities to her person as to render her condition intolerable and thereby has forced her to withdraw from his house and family." She signed her petition "by mark."

Mar. 1, 1813 - Court issued a subpoena for the third Monday of Apr. 1813 for Ulrich Elleberger to appear in court to answer the libel of his wife, Magdalena Elleberger, for a divorce.

Apr. 15, 1813 - Court issued an alias subpoena for Ulrich Elleb-erger to appear in court to answer the libel of his wife, Magdalena Elleberger, for a divorce. Also "April 15th 1813 The death of the Deft. suggested by Abraham Herr."

Lancaster Co., Pa., Appearance Docket Aug. Term 1813 #66 - Christianna Lechler by her next friend, Jacob Fordney, vs. Joseph Lechler, libel in divorce.

Jun. 9, 1813 - Petition of Christiana [sic] Lechler by her uncle and next friend, Jacob Fordney. She married Joseph Lechler in Jan. of 1812. About three months later he abandoned her and took up living loosely with other women. He now "lives in a state of adultery with a certain Catharine Bonnet and contributes nothing to the maintenace [sic] of his said wife."

Jun. 9, 1813 - Court issued a subpoena for Joseph Lechler to appear in court to answer the libel of his wife Christianna Lechler for a divorce.

Aug. 27, 1813 - Court issued an alias subpoena for Joseph Lechler to appear in court to answer the libel of his wife, Christiana Lechler, for a divorce.

Aug. 27, 1813 - Court appointed William B. Ross to take depositions in this case.

Lancaster Co., Pa., Appearance Docket Nov. Term 1813 #43 - Christianna Lechler by her next friend, Jacob Fordney, vs. Joseph Lechler, libel in divorce. Court issued an alias subpoena for Joseph Lechler to appear in court to answer the libel of his wife, Christianna Lechler, for a divorce. Proclamations made Nov. 15, 16, and 17, 1813, for the appearance of Joseph Lechler in court to answer the libel of his wife, Christianna Lechler, for a divorce.

Nov. 17, 1813 - The depositions of Mary Smith, Mary Dieffenderfer, and Michael Teurtac were read and the court granted Christianna Lechler a divorce from her husband, Joseph Lechler. Original documents which include these depositions are missing.

Oct. 5, 1813 - "Evidence on behalf of the Libellant taken before Bird Ross Esquire, Commissioner appointed for that purpose by the court. - Mary Smith, being duly sworn according to law, doth declare and say, that she is well acquainted with Joseph Lechler, and Christianna his wife, the parties to this present libel. That she resides next door to a certain Kitty Bonnet, at the lower end of Queen Street in the borough of Lancaster. That the said Kitty Bonnet lives in a small house, in which there is but one room, and only one bed, and in which house the said Kitty Bonnet has lived and resided since the first Day of April last past. That she has very often since the said first Day of April, seen the Defendant, Joseph Lechler, go in the night-time, into the said Kitty Bonnet's house, and with her the said Kitty, and she has heard them lock the door after them. That she believes the said Joseph Lechler cohabits with the said Kitty Bonnet every night, because she is an early riser, and sees the said Joseph Lechler coming out of the said house almost every morning, frequently only half dressed and carrying water into the house for the said Kitty Bonnett, and has seen him cutting wood for her, making her fires, and making coffee, and cooking breakfast for said Kitty Bonnet. That she has also seen one Henry Hasselbach, come very early to the house and knock at the door, and call the said Joseph out to go to work, when immediately after seen the door opened and the said Joseph come out, bringing his working tools out with him. She has also seen the said Kitty take out dinner to the said Joseph while at work. That she has heard them late in the night conversing together in the house and has also often seen other men coming to the said Kitty's house, and knock at the door, and has immediately after seen the said Joseph come out of the door, and driving them away and that she verily believes from what she has seen and heard, that the said Joseph sleeps in the same bed with the said Kitty

Bonnet, and is in the habit of committing adultery with her and further saith not. Sworn and subscribed before me, this 5th Oct. 1813." Signed by W. B. Ross and Mary Smock "by her mark."

Oct. 5, 1813 - "Michael Teurtoy [sic], being duly sworn according to law doth declare and say that he is well acquainted with the Libellant and the Defendant. That about four months ago, the said Joseph Lechler told this Deponent he would never live with his wife, that he would as soon live with the Devil as with her. Deponent also saith he was present and heard said Joseph Lechler say to Mary Diffenderfer, that he would live and die with his whore. That the said Joseph has often came to the shop where this Deponent was working, to get chips and shaving and Deponent asked him what he was going to do with them. He said they were for his wife. Deponent asked him which wife? He said for his wife Kitty Bonnet. That at another time this Deponent asked him why he did not live with his wife Christiana [sic], he said he would not. I then told him he ought to get a divorce and clear off. He said No. All he waited for was to get her money, and when he got that he would clear off. That this Deponent knows that the said Joseph altogether cohabits with the said Kitty Bonnet, and he has seen them together, at supper, in said Kitty's house and further saith not. Sworn and subscribed before me this 5th Oct. 1813." Signed by W. B. Ross and Michael Teurtor [sic].

Oct. 5, 1813 - "Mary Diffenderfer, being duly sworn according to law, doth declare and say, that she is the mother of the Libellant, Christiana [sic] Lechler, who was intermarried with the Defendant Joseph Lechler, on the 17th January, 1812, in presence of this Deponent. That the said Joseph has left and abandoned the bed and board of his said wife ever since June fair, 1812, although he would frequently come to the house in the day time and abuse the said Deponent and his wife with foul language. That this deponent has frequently told the said Joseph, that she has maintained his wife long enough, and requested him to make some provision for her - but he has refused so to do and makes no provision for her of any sort or kind. That this deponent asked him what was the reason he would not stay with his wife. He said, I never will live with her. I can't stay away from the whore. That about the latter end of May last, he the said Joseph came to the house of this Deponent and behaved very rudely, cursing and swearing and throwing the things about in the kitchen. That she this Deponent spoke civilly to him, and asked him whether or not he meant to live with his wife. He said No, he did not like her, and he could not bear her. He then caught hold of his wife's arm, and threw her out of the kitchen door, and said - By Jesus Christ, I'll live and die with my whore. He also said he did not marry the said Christiana, that he married her money. That this Deponent has not spoken to him since. This Deponent further saith she has often seen the said Joseph and Kitty

Bonnet sitting together at the said Kitty's door, and walking together in the streets - further saith not. Sworn and subscribed this 5th Oct. 1813, before me." Signed by W. B. Ross and Mary Dieffenderfer.

Lancaster Co., Pa., Appearance Docket Nov. Term 1813 #35 - Fanny Lovett by her next friend, States Yentz, vs. Aaron Lovett, libel in divorce. Original action Aug. Term 1813 #36.

Nov. 15, 16, and 17, 1813 - Proclamations made for the appearance of Aaron Lovett to answer the libel of his wife, Fanny Lovett, for a divorce.

Nov. 17, 1813 - Court appointed William B. Ross to take depositions in this case.

Nov. 17, 1813 - Deposition of John Sproat before William B. Ross. He testified that at the time of their marriage, Aaron Lovett and his wife Fanny Lovett lived in Little Brittain Twp., Lancaster Co., Pa. The marriage occured "upwards of nine years past. That upwards of six years since the said Defendant separated himself from his wife, the Plaintiff above named without any just cause known to this deponent and hath continued absent and separate from her ever since according to the best of this deponent's knowledge and belief."

Nov. 18, 1813 - Deposition of John Sproat was read to the court and the court granted Fanny Lovett a divorce from her husband, Aaron Lovett.

Lancaster Co., Pa., Appearance Docket Nov. Term 1813 #36 - Elizabeth Geise by her next friend, John Crommell, vs. Daniel Geise, libel in divorce.

Aug. 28, 1813 - Petition of Elizabeth Geise by her next friend, John Crommell, that she married Daniel Geise Aug. 24, 1809. Her husband deserted her without any just or reasonable cause the very next day. Elizabeth Geise signed her petition "by mark."

Aug. 28, 1813 - The court issued an alias subpoena to Apr. Term 1814 #45 for Daniel Geise to appear in court to answer the libel of his wife, Elizabeth Geise, for a divorce.

Lancaster Co., Pa., Appearance Docket Apr. Term 1814 #45 - Elizabeth Geise by her next friend, John Crommell, vs. Daniel Geise, libel in divorce. Alias subpoena issued for Daniel Geise to appear in court to answer the libel of his wife, Elizabeth Geise, for a divorce. Original documents now missing.

Lancaster Co., Pa., Appearance Docket Nov. Term 1813 #40 - George Axer vs. Barbara Axer, libel in divorce.

Aug. 18, 1813 - Petition of George Axer who testified he married Barbara Newcommer in Mar. of 1805. About nine months later she deserted him without any just or reasonable cause. Petition and affidavit filed.

Aug. 18, 1813 - Court issued a subpoena to Barbara Axer to appear in court to answer the libel of her husband, George Axer, for a divorce.

Lancaster Co., Pa., Appearance Docket Apr. Term 1814 #13 - George Axer vs. Barbara Axer, libel in divorce.

Apr. 18, 1814 - Court issued Barbara Axer an alias subpoena to appear in court to answer the libel of her husband, George Axer, for a divorce.

Apr. 18, 1814 - Court appointed John Hoff, Esq., to take depositions in this case.

Apr. 18, 1814 - Deposition of Michael Axer before John Hoff, Esq., who testified that George and Barbara Axer "were married about eight or nine years past. That they lived together as man and wife for about the space of one year according to the best of Deponents knowledge. That the said Barbara, the Defendant above named, then seperated [sic] herself from the said George, the Plaintiff above named, without any just or reasonable cause according (to) the best of this deponent's (knowledge) and hath continued seperate [sic] ever since."

Apr. 23, 1814 - Deposition of Michael Axer, Jr., read to the court and the court granted George Axer a divorce from his wife Barbara Axer.

Lancaster Co., Pa., Appearance Docket Jan. Term 1814 #14 - Mary Lions by her next friend, William Eberman, vs. Thomas Lions, libel in divorce.

Nov. 12, 1813 - Petition of Mary Lions by her next friend, William Eberman, stated that she married Thomas Lions in May of 1800. She had lived seven years and upwards in Pa. Her husband deserted her in Sept. of 1806. Mary Lions signed her petition "Mary Lyons."

Nov. 16, 1813 - Court issued a subpoena to Thomas Lions to appear in court to answer the libel of his wife, Mary Lions, for a divorce. Affidavit and petition were filed.

Lancaster Co., Pa., Appearance Docket Apr. Term 1814 #16 - Mary Lions by her next friend, William Eberman, vs. Thomas Lions, libel in divorce.

Apr. 18, 1814 - Court appointed John Hoff to take depositions.

Apr. 26, 1814 - Deposition of John Riddle before John Hoff in the borough of Lancaster. "John Riddle of the age of 58 and upwards being duly sworn deposeth and saith that he knew Mary Lions the Complainant and Thomas Lions the Defendant about twelve or thirteen years and that they then lived in the Borough of Lancaster in the County of Lancaster and State of Pennsylvania in a married state and that between seven and eight years ago the said Thomas Lions left her and has not cohabited with her since or been seen or heard of in the Borough of Lancaster and that he left her with three small children which she has supported ever since by her industry and further he saith not." (Talk about a run-on sentence!!)

Apr. 29, 1814 - Deposition of John Riddle was read to the court and the court granted Mary Lions a divorce from her husband Thomas Lions.

Lancaster Co., Pa., Appearance Docket Apr. Term 1814 #14 - Elizabeth Shoneberger by her next friend, Amos Gaylord, vs. Peter Shoneberger, libel in divorce.

Jan. 24, 1814 - Petition of Elizabeth Shoneberger by her next friend, Amos Gaylord, who said that about twenty fur [sic] years ago she married Peter Shoneberger. About eight years ago her husband deserted her without any just or reasonable cause.

Jan. 24, 1814 - Court issued a subpoena for Peter Shoneberger to appear in court to answer the libel of his wife, Elizabeth Shoneberger, for a divorce. Petition and affidavit filed.

Lancaster Co., Pa., Appearance Docket Aug. Term 1814 #36 - Elizabeth Shoeneberger [sic] by her next friend, Amos Gaylord, vs. Peter Shoeneberger [sic], libel in divorce.

Aug. 26, 1814 - Court issued an alias subpoena to Peter Shoeneberger [sic] to answer the libel of his wife, Elizabeth Shoeneber [sic], for a divorce.

Aug. 26, 1814 - Court appointed William Child, Esq., to take depositions in this case.

Sept. 29, 1814 - Deposition of George Beiler who testified that he knew both parties in this case. Peter Shoeneberger [sic] "left his wife upwards of eight years ago and that he hath not returned to live with her." George Beiler signed his deposition "by mark."

Sept. 29, 1814 - Deposition of Sarah Beiler who testified that she lived near Peter Shoeneberger [sic] in Huntingdon Co., Pa., and was well acquainted with him and his wife Elizabeth. Peter Shoeneberger [sic] left his wife upwards of eight years ago and didn't return. Sarah Beiler signed her deposition "by mark."

Nov. 28, 1814 - The court granted Elizabeth Shoeneberger [sic] a divorce from her husband, Peter Shoeneberger [sic].

Lancaster Co., Pa., Appearance Docket Apr. Term 1814 #74 - Christian Miller vs. Elizabeth Miller, libel in divorce.

Mar. 18, 1814 - Petition of Christian Miller who has lived in Pa., upwards of fifteen years. He married his present wife, Elizabeth on Aug. 28, 1787. She deserted him on or about Jul. 29, 1810, and "went to reside amongst her sister and friends in the County of Lancaster." Since then she has committed adultery with Jacob Sherick and has had a bastard child.

Mar. 22, 1814 - Court issued a subpoena to Elizabeth Miller to appear in court and answer the libel of her husband, Christian Miller, for a divorce. It was to be served by a copy left at the homes of John Davis and John Kaufman.

Apr. 26, 1814 - Court appointed Ignatius Lighter, Esq., of the borough of York, and Israel Lloyd, Esq., of Lancaster Co., Pa., to take depositions in this case.

Apr. 27, 1814 - "on motion of Mr. Rogers in behalf of Defendant, a rule for the Plaintiff Christian Miller to show cause why the Libel and Proceedings should not be quashed, Mar. 20th, 1816 argued, Rule discharged."

Lancaster Co., Pa., Appearance Docket Aug. Term 1814 #37 - Christian Miller vs. Elizabeth Miller, libel in divorce.

Aug. 16, 1814 - Deposition of Elizabeth Miller before Samuel Carpenter. She contested the libel of her husband Christian Miller. She married her husband in Aug. of 1787. Her husband prosecuted her for adultery by libel of Aug. 19, 1813. By trial by jury held Jan. 21, 1814, she was found innocent. About Apr. 1, 1812, Christian Miller committed adultery with Eve Millet and continued "to commit adultery" with her until the first part of Apr. 1814. Elizabeth Miller signed her deposition "by mark."

Nov. 25, 1814 - Court appointed Samuel Carpenter, Esq., to take depositions in this case.

Jan. 24, 1815 - Plaintiff filed an application to have arbitrators chosen Feb. 14, 1815.

Feb. 14, 1815 - Prothonotary choose George Matter, Esq., John Light, Esq., and Mathias Young as arbitrators to meet in the house of John Michael in Lancaster, Pa., Mar. 14, 1815, at 10 o'clock A.M.

March 15, 1815 - "Report of the arbitrators filed stating that in their opinion the notice of the meeting of the arbitrators was not legally served on the Defendant and that it is also their opinion that they have no jurisdiction in this case."

Lancaster Co., Pa., Appearance Docket Aug. Term 1814 #75 - Conrad Engle vs. Barbara Engle, libel in divorce.

Jun. 2, 1814 - Petition of Conrad Engle of Warwick Twp., Lancaster Co., Pa., a native citizen of Pa. He married his present wife, Barbara, in 1798. He accused her of "the henious sin of adultery." His petition was signed "by mark."

Jun. 2, 1814 - Petition and affidavit filed and the court issued an subpoena for Barbara Engle to appear in court to answer the libel of her husband, Conrad Engle, for a divorce.

Aug. 16, 1814 - Court appointed Peter Lehnart, Esq., of Warwick Twp., Lancaster Co., Pa., to take deposition in this case.

Aug. 16, 1814 - The court issued an alias subpoena to Barbara Engle to appear in court to answer the libel of her husband, Conrad Engle, for a divorce.

Lancaster Co., Pa., Appearance Docket Nov. Term 1814 #131 - Conrad Engle vs. Barbara Engle, libel in divorce.

Aug. 16, 1814 - Court issued an alias subpoena to Barbara Engle to appear in court to answer the libel of her husband, Conrad Engle, for a divorce. Sheriff reported he served this subpoena and it took him twelve miles to do this.

Aug. 16, 1814 - Court appointed Peter Lenhart, Esq., to take depositions in this case.

Oct. 8, 1814 - Deposition of George Engle. "He was present when Conrad Engle upbraided his late wife Barbara with having been at the house of Philip Kile, Innkeeper, on Easter Monday the eleventh day of April last past, and that the said Barbara had taken Samuel Banner with her to the house of Christian Becker, Junior (where she then had her home.) She at first denied it, whereupon Conrad asked whether she would swear he had not gone with her. She answered she could not swear that he had not gone a part of the road with her. (It was late at night when he had been with her, and the said Banner bears a very indefant [sic] character, among chaste people.) This deponent further heard the said Conrad and Barbara have a dispute about her first child with which she was pregnant and before their marriage and which she laid to the charge of said Conrad, when she openly confessed the said Conrad was not the father, and though she had outwardly sworn the same to him yet in her heart she at the same time swore on Henry Myer (by whose name it at present goes). This deponent more than a half dozen times heard her say (without assigning any cause) she would never in her life live with Conrad Engle any more - and further this deponent saith not. "

Oct. 8, 1814 - Deposition of Philip Kile who saw on Easter Monday "Samuel Banner and Barbara Engle standing together at the door of his home - to the best of this affirmant's recollection it was then about eleven o'clock at night."

Oct. 8, 1814 - Deposition of Henry Hohwerter who in the autumn of 1813 was at the house of Michael Kline where Barbara Engle then made her home. He saw Barbara Engle sitting on the knees of a man named Jackson. She left that place not longer after that to be "free with the men." He was at the house of Philip Kile last Easter Monday and saw Barbara Engle leave the house about midnight. At the same time Samuel Bauer was also missing.

Oct. 8, 1814 - Deposition of Elizabeth Shiffer who was employed by Conrad and Barbara Engle to spin wool at their house. She heard Barbara Engle abuse her husband and say she would no longer live with him. "This deponent frequently heard him make use of the kindest language to her, praying her to behave and live with him as a good wife should do, but she absolutely refused and said she would leave him and never live with him anymore in her life. This deponent herself expostulated with her and entreated her as a friend to do so but all to no purpose. She said she would never live with him any more. When he found she was fixed in her mind he had no other way left to sell of his goods and give up housekeeping altogether. When he had already mounted his horse to ride to the vender Cryer, he once more spoke to her in mild terms asking her to live with him at the same time telling her if she would, he would not say a word about all that that had ever passed between them. But she obstinately refused - nevertheless before he made vendue he gave her household and kitchen furniture sufficent to keep house besides some provisions. She frequently while with him in her passion - reproached him about a certain Margaret Miller saying she believed he thought more of her than of his wife. Although this deponent is convinced, she did not believe it herself, and that it was merely a pretext to leave him. The said Margaret Miller is a woman that has daughters married to respectable men, and has grandchildren. She maintains herself by working for other people both in and out of the house and is frequently employed by almost every respectable family in the parts both far and near, and the said Barbara being sick (or pretending so to be as she is known to have done more than once) intreated [sic] her said husband to get the said Margaret to attend and nurse her which he thereupon did for a few days to satisfy her. Since the said Barbara left her husband, this deponent saw her at the house of Philip Kile sitting on the knees of a certain Samuel Bauer and behaving in a manner more becoming a lewd woman than an honest or married one - Further this Deponent saith not." Elizabeth Shiffer signed her deposition "by mark."

Nov. 24, 1814 -Court appointed William B. Ross of the borough of Lancaster, Pa., to take depositions in this case.

Nov. 24, 1814 - The deposition of John Ners said he was present at conversation between Conrad Engle and his wife Barbara. "Conrad charged her with having criminal and carnal connection with another man of the name of Samuel Bower. She said she could not deny but she had connection with him and that he had bragged of it, or she would never told it, but she said she would never live any more with her husband and further saith not."

Nov. 24, 1814 - The court granted Conrad Engle a divorce from his wife Barbara Engle.

Lancaster Co., Pa., Appearance Docket Aug. Term 1814 #111 - Catharine Wilson by her next friend, Peter Nagle, vs. Joseph Wilson, libel in divorce.

Jun. 3, 1814 - Petition of Catharine Wilson by her next friend, Peter Nagle, before John Hoff, Esq. She testified that she married Joseph Wilson Nov. 12, 1807. She accused him of adultery and that he deserted her without any just cause about "a year last past."

Jun. 10, 1814 - Court issued a subpoena for Joseph Wilson to appear in court to answer the libel of his wife, Catharine Wilson, for a divorce. Subpoena was served by copy and the sheriff charged for twelve miles to do it.

Aug. 22, 1814 - Court appointed William Child, Esq., to take depositions in this case.

Lancaster Co., Pa., Appearance Docket Nov. Term 1814 #67 - Catharine Wilson by her next friend, Peter Nagle, vs. Joseph Wilson, libel in divorce. Alias subpoena served by copy and the sheriff charged for twelve miles. Contd. to Apr. Term 1818. Original documents missing.

Lancaster Co., Pa., Appearance Docket Jan. Term 1815 #2 - Jane Barkman vs. John Barkman, libel in divorce. Sheriff reported he traveled twelve miles to serve the subpoena in divorce.
Jan. 28, 1815 - Rule to take depositions. Contd. term to term until Jun. 4, 1816 - William C. Frazee, Esq., atttorney for libellant moved the court to withdraw the libel for divorce and alimony which was resisted by Mr. Hopkins, Council for the Respondent. Motion granted by the court.

Lancaster Co., Pa., Appearance Docket Apr. Term 1815 #65 - Rebecca Cochran by her next friend, John Smith, vs. Oliver Cochran, libel for alimony.
Jan. 23, 1815 - "The petition of Rebecca Cochran, wife of Oliver Cochran, of Donegal Township, Carpenter, humbly showeth that your petitioner hath at all times since her intermarriage with the said Oliver, in every respect behaved herself towards him as a good and faithful wife ought to do. That the said Oliver for a considerable time past hath been in the habitual practice of drunkeness [sic] and neglected to provide your petitioner a competent maintenance and support. Your petitioner therefore prays your Honors to cause the said Oliver to appear and give surity for such suitable provisions and support as your Honors may deem meet. And she will ever pray. - (signed) Rebecca Cochran."
Jan. 23, 1815 - Court issued a subpoena to Oliver Cochran to appear in court to answer the libel of his wife, Rebecca Cochran, for alimony. Sheriff reported it took him thirteen miles to serve this subpoena.
Apr. 25, 1815 - Court appointed William Childs, Esq., to take depositions in this case. Contd. to Apr. 1818 Term.

Lancaster Co., Pa., Appearance Docket Aug. Term 1815 #52 - George Rank vs. Elizabeth Rank, libel in divorce.
Apr. 18, 1815 - Petition of George Rank of Earl Twp., Lancaster Co., Pa., who testified that he married his present wife Elizabeth on Jun. 12, 1809. She deserted him without any just or reasonable cause in Nov. of 1809.
Apr. 18, 1815 - Court issued a subpoena to Elizabeth Rank to appear in court to answer the libel of her husband, George Rank, for a divorce.
Sept. 2, 1815 - Court appointed Matthias Shirk, Esq., to take depositions in this case.

Dec. 1, 1815 - Deposition of Barbara Hummell before Matthias Shirk who testified that Elizabeth Rank left her husband about five years ago and never returned. She didn't know where she now lives. Barbara Hummel signed her deposition "by mark."

Dec. 2, 1815 - Deposition of Barbara Hummel was read to the court, and the court granted George Rank a divorce from his wife, Elizabeth Rank.

Lancaster Co., Pa., Appearance Docket Nov. Term 1815 #126 - George Rank vs. Elizabeth Rank, libel in divorce. Original documents now missing (perhaps placed with Aug. Term 1815 #53).

Lancaster Co., Pa., Appearance Docket Nov. Term 1815 #125 - John Underwood vs. Sarah Underwood, libel in divorce.

Aug. 22, 1815 - Petition of John Underwood of Leacock Twp., Lancaster Co., Pa. He married his present wife, Sarah, in May of 1802 and she deserted him without, any just or reasonable cause over four years ago.

Aug. 22, 1815 - Court issued a subpoena to Sarah Underwood to appear in court to answer the libel of her husband, John Underwood, for a divorce.

Nov. 20, 1815 - Court appointed William Barton, Esq., to take depositions in this case.

Lancaster Co., Pa., Appearance Docket Apr. Term 1816 #2 - John Underwood vs. Sarah Underwood, libel in divorce. Sheriff Hambright returned that he caused public notice of divorce to be given in the *Lancaster Journal* for four successive weeks. Depositions of Samuel Gerber and Henry Gerber were read and John Underwood was granted a divorce from his wife Sarah Underwood, Apr. 16, 1816. Original documents are now missing.

Lancaster Co., Pa., Appearance Docket Nov. Term 1815 #205 - Catharine Lowell by her next friend, Michael Dochterman, vs. George Lowell, libel in divorce.

Oct. 13, 1815 - Petition of Catharine Lowell, a native of Pa., aged over twenty-one years of age. She married in the winter of 1810 George Lowell who deserted her without any just reason or cause in Mar. of 1811. Both Catharine Lowell and Michael Dochterman signed "by mark."

Oct. 13, 1815 - Court issued a subpoena to George Lowell to appear in court to answer the libel of his wife, Catharine Lowell, for a divorce.

Jan. 22, 1816 - Court appointed William Barton, Esq., to take depositions.

Lancaster Co., Pa., Appearance Docket Apr. Term 1816 #152 - Catharine Lowell by her next friend, Michael Dochterman, vs. George Lowell, libel in divorce. Sheriff returned that he had public notice of divorce published in the *Lancaster Journal* for four successive weeks.

Mar. 10, 1816 - Court appointed William Barton, Esq., to take depositions in this case.

Mar. 19, 1816 - Deposition of Abraham Hernley, farmer of Mt. Joy Twp., Lancaster Co., Pa., and Adam Keener of Rapho Twp., Lancaster Co., Pa. Abraham Hernley lived about a half mile from where the Lowells were married and lived. They were married in Feb. or Mar. of 1810. The morning after the marriage George Lowell stopped at his house and told him of his marriage. He saw them together after that and they seemed to be on good terms. About two months after the marriage George went to the states of Deleware and Jersey. He got a letter from him dated May 15, 1810, Bridgewater, New Jersey, expressing his intention of returning and included an affectionate part for his wife which he read to her. He was told that in the summer of 1810, George returned and spent an hour or two at his mother-in-laws where his wife was staying. Adam Keener testified he lived in the same house with George and Catharine Lowell during part of the time after they were married. George left his wife without any just cause. He came back and stayed only about one hour and did not show much tenderness or affection for his wife. Adam Keener signed "by mark."

Apr. 16, 1816 - Depositions of Abraham Hernley and Adam Keener were read and the court granted Catharine Lowell a divorce from her husband, George Lowell.

Lancaster Co., Pa., Appearance Docket Apr. Term 1816 #106 - Sarah Seglesmith by her next friend, John Heiss, vs. Frederick Seglesmith, libel in divorce.

Nov. 4, 1815 - Petition of Sarah Seglesmith that she married Frederick Seglesmith in Dec. of 1808. He deserted her in Jul. of 1811 without any just reason or cause.

Lancaster Co., Pa., Appearance Docket Aug. Term 1816 #109 - Sarah Seglesmith by her next friend, John Heiss, vs. Frederick Seglesmith, libel in divorce.

Apr. 20, 1816 - Court appointed William Martin to take depositions in this case.

Jun. 12, 1816 - Deposition of John Tobias Heiss of the borough of Lancaster, Pa., house carpenter, and brother of Sarah Seglesmith. His sister Sarah was married seven or eight years ago in the borough of Lancaster to Frederick Seglesmith. They lived together about one year "during which time their only child, a boy now nearly seven years of age was born." About five days after his birth, Frederick Seglesmith deserted his wife without any just or reasonable cause.

Jun. 12, 1816 - Deposition of Caroline Reinhart and Mary Grubb who testified that they knew Sarah Seglesmith long before her marriage as they were neighbors. Sarah was married between seven and eight years ago. Sarah and her husband lived together about a year and had a son. Her husband then deserted her. Mary Grubb signed her deposition "by mark."

Aug. 19, 1816 - Sheriff George Hambright reported that notice was given in the *Lancaster Journal* for four successive weeks. The depositions of John Tobias Heiss, Caroline Reinhart, and Mary Grubb were read to the court whereupon the court granted Sarah Seglesmith a divorce from her husband Frederick Seglesmith.

Lancaster Co., Pa., Appearance Docket Aug. Term 1816 #108 - Margaret Shuman by her next friend, Daniel Ehler, vs. Peter Shuman, libel in divorce.

Apr. 17, 1816 - Petition of Margaret Shuman that she married Peter Shuman on Mar. 4, 1808. He deserted her without any just cause or reason on Aug. 24, 1812.

Apr. 19, 1816 - Court issued a subpoena for Peter Shuman to appear in court to answer the libel of his wife, Margaret Shuman, for a divorce.

Lancaster Co., Pa., Appearance Docket Nov. Term 1816 #60 - Margaret Shuman by her next friend, Daniel Echler, vs. Peter Shuman, libel in divorce.

Aug. 27, 1817 -Sheriff reported that he gave public notice to Peter Shuman in the *Lancaster Journal* for four successive weeks and the court appointed John Light to take depositions in this case.

Sept. 24, 1816 - Deposition of Margaret Fooes of the borough of Lancaster who was well acquainted with Peter and Margaret Shuman. Peter Shuman left his wife in Aug. of 1812 without any reasonable cause known to her. Margaret Fooes signed her deposition "by mark."

Sept. 25, 1816 - Deposition of Susannah Backenstose of the borough of Lancaster, widow, well acquainted with Peter and Margaret Shuman as they lived in the same house. Peter Shuman left his wife in Aug. of 1812 without reasonable cause. Susannah Backenstose signed her deposition "by mark."

Sept. 28, 1816 - Deposition of Margaret Bush of the borough of Lancaster who was well acquainted with Peter and Margaret Shuman. Peter Shuman left his wife in Aug. of 1812 without reasonable cause. She is certain as to the time he deserted "as her brother at that time enlisted in the Army of the United States." Margaret Bush signed her deposition "by mark."

Nov. 22, 1816 - Depositions of Margaret Foose, Susannah Backenstose, and Margaret Bush were read to the court and the court granted Margaret Shuman a divorce from her husband, Peter Shuman.

Lancaster Co., Pa., Appearance Docket Nov. Term 1816 #58 - Catharine Giddens by her next friend, Joshua Nicholason, vs. James Giddens, libel in divorce.

Aug. 17, 1816 - Petition of Catharine Giddens of the borough of

Lancaster who married James Giddens in Jul. of 1809. "Your petitioner was obliged by the violent and outrageous conduct of her said husband towards her to escape from his house and seek shelter in the hospital of the County aforesaid and where in consequence of his last assult [sic] upon her she was confined to a sick bed for and during the period of one month. During this confinement she contracted necessarily a considerable debt - the liquidation of which obliged your libellant to labor a long time in said establishment, as a servant, her husband refusing and entirely neglecting to advance money in her support. Since the year Eighteen Hundred Fifteen your petitioner admits she has absented herself from the said James entirely, believing herself justified in so doing by his abusive conduct and unhusbandlike behavior at the period alluded to and your libellant further sheweth that from an early period after her intermarriage with said James until the year last above mentioned, she had frequently been forced by his threats and beatings to escape for her life at the dreary hour of midnight from his merciless hand and seek the protection of her neighbors and your petitioner further represents to your Honor that said James - returning from his nightly revels intoxicated, would seize with brutal vialance [sic] and beat without provacation [sic] in the most inhuman manner the only pledge of his former affection - their infant child. Moreover your libellant declared that she had not received from said James any support or aid - direct or indirect for herself or child for the last two years his habits of intemperance rendering her illy [sic] disposed to labour and consequently unable to afford her acquantance [sic]." Catharine Giddens signed her petition "by mark."

Lancaster Co., Pa., Appearance Docket Jan. Term 1817 #184 - Catharine Giddens by her next friend, Joshua Nicholson, vs. James Giddens, libel in divorce.

Jan. 24, 1817 - Court appointed William Barton, Esq., to take depositions in this case. Original documents are now missing.

Lancaster Co., Pa., Appearance Docket Nov. Term 1816 #59 - Mary Hopkins by her next friend, Jonathan Hinkle, vs. William Hopkins, libel in divorce. Original documents are now missing.

Lancaster Co., Pa., Appearance Docket Jan. Term 1817 #23 - Mary Hopkins by her next friend, Jonathan Hinkle, vs. William Hopkins, libel in divorce.

Jan. 22, 1817 - Court appointed William Barton, Esq., to take depositions in this case. Defendant says his wife deserted him and plaintiff denied she did so. Contd. term to term until Jan. 1819.

Feb. 17, 1819 - Jury trial ruled for the respondent.

Feb. 17, 1819 - Sr. Buchanan requested a new trial.

Feb. 18, 1819 - Libellant appeared to Supreme Court. Original documents in this case are now missing.

Lancaster Co., Pa., Appearance Docket Nov. Term 1816 #157 - Margaret Patrick by her next friend, John McClure, vs. John Patrick, libel in divorce.

Sept. 19, 1816 - Petition of Margaret Patrick who married John Patrick on Nov. 9, 1804. "Yet so it is that the said John Patrick did at or about the month of August in the year of our Lord One Thousand Eight Hundred and Fourteen and for some time previous therto, so cruelly and barbarously treat and endanger the life, and offer such indignities to the person of your libellant, as to render her condition intolerable and life burdensome and thereby forced her, your libellant, in the month of August aforesaid (1814) to withdraw from his house and family in which she has never since returned, nor as your libellant firmly believes could she safely do so.

Sept. 23, 1816 - Court issued a subpoena for John Patrick to appear in court to answer the libel of his wife, Margaret Patrick, for a divorce.

Lancaster Co., Pa., Appearance Docket Jan. Term 1817 #107 - Margaret Patrick by her next friend, John McClure, vs. John Patrick, libel in divorce.

Apr. 22, 1817 - Deposition of Hannah Coil. "She was present and saw John Patrick take hold of his wife Margaret Patrick by the hair and abuse her in a most inhuman manner. That he beat her until the blood ran out of her fact. That he took her cloaths [sic] and burnt [sic] them. That he broke the spinning wheel, the only thing by which she could at that time make a living and burned it in the stove. Then he turned her out of his house and used her so badly, that this deponent believes that if she the said Margaret had not left him he would have taken her life. That he was frequently drunk and often sold property for the sake of getting money for the purpose of buying drink. That this conduct was often repeated and for a length of time for at least eighteen months." Hannah Coil signed her deposition "by mark."

Apr. 22, 1817 - Deposition of Eleanor Harkins, of the borough of Lancaster, widow. She lived in the same house as John Patrick and his wife, Margaret, for one year, about five years ago. "That, within that time, she this deponent had frequent opportunities of witnessing the harsh and cruel treatment of the said Margaret Patrick by her said Husband, at sometimes by pulling at her, when she was bloody in consequence thereof, by burning her spinning wheel, by using opprobrious language to her and by otherwise maltreating her. That after the said John Patrick had left Mrs. Coil's house and removed to Bethell's Town, viz about two years and nine months ago, his said wife Margaret came to the home of her this Deponent in an evening, and after the Deponent had gone to bed and requested admittance, saying that her husband threatened her life, that he had something that would do for her, that she this Deponent admitted her accordingly, and she the said Margaret remained with her all night and part of the next day, appearing to be afraid to go home. That the said Margaret came at other times to her house, in the night, making similiar [sic] complaints of the ill treatment of her by her husband and of her fear of her life in consequence thereof. That so far as she this Deponent had an opporunity [sic] of offering and knowing, the conduct of the said Margaret Patrick toward her husband was that of an industrious, careful, good wife, giving no provacation [sic] for her husband's inhuman treatment of her. Further she this Deponent saith not." Eleanor Harkins signed her deposition "by mark."

Lancaster Co., Pa., Appearance Docket Aug. Term 1817 #20 - Susanna Correll by her next friend, Frederick Stouffer, vs. David Correll, libel in divorce.

Mar. 28, 1817 - Petition of Susanna Correll by her next friend Frederick Stouffer before Samuel Carpenter, Justice of the peace. Susanna married David Correll about "twenty years past." He abused her and endangered her life forcing her to leave him about ten years ago. Susanna Correll signed her petition "by mark."

Apr. 22, 1817 - Court issued a subpoena to David Correll to appear in court to answer the libel of his wife, Susanna Correll, for a divorce.

Lancaster Co., Pa., Appearance Docket Nov. Term 1817 #69 - Susanna Correll by her next friend, Frederick Stouffer, vs. David Correll, libel in divorce.

Jan. 27, 1818 - Court appointed Samuel Carpenter, Esq., to take depositions in this case.

Mar. 27, 1818 - Deposition of John Stouffer - "Personally appeared before me one of the subscribed Commissioners appointed to take depositions in the above cause John Stouffer who being duly affirmed according to law doth declare and says that he is well acquainted with the above named Susanna Correll and David Correll and knows that they lived together as man and wife and had several children and that the said David Correll has willfully and maliciously deserted the said Susanna his wife without reasonable cause for and during the term and space of two years and further saith not."

Mar. 27, 1818 - Deposition of John Hess - "Personally appeared before me the subscribed Commissioner appointed to take depositions in the above case John Hess who being duly affirmed according to law doth declare and say that he is well acquainted with the above named Susanna Correll and David Correll and knows that they lived together as husband and wife and had several children and that the said David Correll willfully and maliciously deserted the said Susanna his wife without reasonable cause for and during the term and space of two years and further saith not."

Apr. 14, 1818 - Depositions of John Stouffer and John Hess were read to the court. Proof was presented that notice was placed four successive weeks in the *Lancaster Journal* whereupon the court granted Susanna Correll a divorce from her husband David Correll.

Lancaster Co., Pa., Appearance Docket Aug. Term 1817 #21 - Catharine Haines by her next friend, Rosina Sheller, vs. Daniel Haines, the younger, libel in divorce.

Apr. 25, 1817 - Petition of Catharine Haines by her next friend Rosina Sheller. She married Daniel Haines, the younger, May 13, 1810. He deserted her without cause and for the last five years and upwards "entered into wanton dispolute [*sic*] and adulterous practices with other woman [*sic*]". Catharine Haines said she was born in Pa., and had always lived there. Catharine Haines signed her name to the petition but Rosina Sheller signed "by mark."

Apr. 25, 1817 - The Court issued a subpoena to Daniel Haines, the younger, to appear in court to answer the libel of his wife, Catharine Haines, for a divorce.

Aug. 30, 1817 - Court appointed John Hoff, Esq., to take depositions in this case.

Nov. 27, 1817 - Deposition of Philip Eberman who on Apr. 28th 1817 took Daniel Haines, Jr., on virtue of a state warrant on complaint of Sarah Hughs for fornication and bastardy. "When he brought the said Daniel Haines, Jr. before the Esquire, he acknowledged that he was guilty and that he did not deny that the child belonged to him, and that he was the father of the child."

Nov. 27, 1817 - Deposition of George Koenig who testified that Daniel Haines, Jr., left his wife in Mar. of 1811 and has not lived with her or provided for her ever since.

Nov. 27, 1817 - Deposition of John Wind that Daniel Haines, Jr., left his wife and child in Mar. or Apr. of 1811 and did not live with her or provide for her ever since.

Nov. 27, 1817 - Depositions of Philip Eberman, George Koenig, and John Wind were read to the court and the court granted Catharine Haines a divorce from her husband, Daniel Haines, the younger.

Lancaster Co., Pa., Appearance Docket Nov. Term 1817 #47 - Catharine Haines by her next friend, Rosina Sheller, vs. Daniel Haines, the younger, libel in divorce.

Oct. 15, 1817 - Court appointed William B. Ross to take depositions in this case.

Nov. 17, 1817 - Court recorded the appointment of William B. Ross to take depositions in this case. Original documents are now missing.

Lancaster Co., Pa., Appearance Docket Aug. Term 1817 #22 - Maria Kellheffer former Geiter by her next friend, John Markley, vs. Christian Kellheffer, libel in divorce.

Apr. 21, 1817 - Petition of Maria Kellheffer, formerly Geiter by her next friend, John Markley, for divorce and alimony from Christian

Kellheffer. They were married Oct. 25, 1807. He abused her and endangered her life causing her to leave him Feb. 1, 1816. She signed her petition "by mark."

Apr. 22, 1817 - Court issued a subpoena to Christian Kellheffer to appear in court to answer the libel of his wife, Maria Kellheffer, for a divorce. Defendant denies that he mistreated his wife.

Sept. 17, 1817 - "The Court are of opinion that the proofs produced are not sufficient to entitle the libellant to a divorce."

Oct. 13, 1820 - Maria Kellheffer requests a jury trial in her libel for a divorce from her husband, Christian Kellheffer.

Nov. 22, 1820 - Court appointed Samuel Carpenter, Esq., to take depositions in this case at his Lancaster, Pa., office Monday Dec. 4, 1820, between 10 o'clock forenoon and 4 o'clock in the afternoon.

Dec. 4, 1820 - Deposition of Robert Jones who was acquainted with Christian and Maria Kellheffer about twenty years. "That the said Christian frequently employed deponant [sic] for mowing, and when they came to the table, for their meals, the said Christian began quarreling with his wife, the said Mary [sic], about the vituals [sic] which did not please him. That the deponant [sic] found no fault with the vituals [sic], that they were cooked well, and were not only good, but served nice and clean, on the table. One morning in perticular [sic], there was a quarrel between the said Christian and Mary, but about what they quarreled, defendant [sic] did not know, but amongst their quarrel aforesaid, the said Christian said that he would be dammed if he would not brake [sic] every bone in the body of his wife the said Mary [sic], that before long - said deponant [sic] further saith that he helped the said Christian to gather apples, make cider and broil applebutter. In the morning when the applebutter was to be broiled, the deponent came early to the house of the said Christian, when he arrived at the house, Christian was not up, the deponant [sic] nocked [sic] at the door, and Christian let him in, dressed himself, and when he went to see about the fire, there was none at his Christian's house. He, the said Christian, then went to the house where his wife the said Mary [sic] (for they did not sleep in the same house) and found her the said Mary's [sic] door fast, he the said Christian without calling out to the said Mary [sic], to open the house for him, went and got a piece of scoutling [sic] and forced the door open, but found no fire in her house. He the said Christian, then went to a neighbor's house for fire. While the said Christian was gone for fire, the said Mary [sic] came out and inquired what was the cause of such violence, saying that if the said Christian called on her, that she would have opened the door for him, notwithstanding he the said Christian does not sleep in the same house with her. Deponent further saith, that himself and the said Christian then kindled a fire, put the cider over and broiled the applebutter, but the said Mary [sic] was not suffered to help at cooking the said applebutter, tho [sic] she offered her services, but was refused by the said Christian any further than to put the applebutter out of the kettle unto the earthen pots, for which the said Mary [sic] again offered her services, and was then permitted to her from that part. And deponent further saith that one rainy morning he called on the said Christian for the lone [sic] of his fishing rod hook and line to fish with, which he got the lone [sic] of and then spent the whole or nearly the whole day fishing. When he brought him the said fishing impliments [sic], the said Christian was setting right in the door where the said Mary [sic] kept her bread. Mary [sic] then there said she was glad that defendant [sic] came, for if nobody had came she could not have got her bread for supper that night. The deponent then asked Mary [sic] why she could not get her supper, she then replied that Christian her husband was setting in the door where the bread is kept, and swears that if she would offer to cross there that he would take her life. The said Mary [sic] then went in and got bread, and as she went past the said Christian, while deponant [sic] had his eyes turned away from them, Mary said to Christian, 'Are you going to begin on me in the presence of strangers, when Robert is here?' But deponant [sic] did not see the said Christian treat his said wife Mary [sic]. The said Mary [sic] then asked deponant to take supper with her, which he declined to take, untill [sic] the said Christian invited him to supper. He then sat down and took supper. After supper was over, deponant [sic] made reply and said that he would go home. The said Mary [sic] then said for God's Sake do not go home for I am in danger of my life. Deponant [sic] then replied that if she the said Mary [sic] was in danger of her life, he would stay and did stay. The same Mary [sic] then told him that the said Christian had threatened her life through the whole day. Deponant [sic] slept in the same house with the said Christian. In the morning deponant [sic] got up bid farewell and went home, and nothing further took place that night to the knowledge of the deponant [sic]. When the said Mary [sic] made the complaints aforesaid, the said Christian made no reply. The foregoing circumstances took place upwards of five years ago. Said deponent [sic] further saith that to the best of his knowledge, the foregoing statement contains all he knows and recolects [sic] about those circumstances and further saith not." Robert Jones signed his deposition "by mark."

Dec. 4, 1820 - Deposition of "Christian Eshleman being duly affirmed according to law, saith that he is acquainted with Christian Kelhaefler [sic] and Mary [sic] his wife the parties in this suit for about seven years. That he frequently heard the said Christian complain of his wife, that she cooked or fried his sausages to [sic] rich that he did not like to eat them that way, in consequence whereof he had to fry his own sausages himself and showed affirmant how he cooked them on the stove, and also shewed [sic] him then that the said Mary [sic] cooked, however them that the said Mary [sic] cooked had a better appearance than those that Christian cooked. And that he several times saw the said Christian take his meals before the door, when affirmant inquired into the cause of his so doing Christian's reply was that it was his wife's fault, that he must cook for himself and affirmant further saith that he one time caught or ealth [sic] saw the said Christian milking his cows, when affirmant went into the barn of his so doing, he replied that if his wife the said Mary [sic] milked the cows she would sell the produce thereof, and put away or give the same to her friends. That the said Mary's [sic] mother was a devil, to whom the produce of the milk was applied, and that he would sooner milk the cows himself and give the milk to the Hogs, which would do some good, otherwise if the wife the said Mary [sic] milks the cows, he gets no use thereof. Affirmant further saith that the said Mary [sic] called on him the affirmant and informed him that she was in fear of her life to live with her husband. That he was a very bad man, that he kept several guns and a large club about his house, that she was in fear that her said husband would take her life with the said two guns and club. But affirmant did not see the said Christian offer to do any harm to the said Mary [sic]. That at another time, he saw the said Mary [sic] dabbed with eggs that she said the said Christian had done by threwing [sic] her with eggs. And another time he saw her with a bloody nose now which the said Mary [sic] said her husband the said Christian had given her, by striking her, but affirmant never saw the said Christian offer any personal violence to the said Mary [sic] and further saith not."

Dec. 4, 1820 - Deposition of "John Galligher being duly sworn according to law saith, that he is acquainted with Christian Kelhaeffer [sic] the Defendant in their suit, for about seventeen years and with Mary [sic] Kelheffer [sic] (formerly Geiter) since she is married to the said Christian Kelheffer [sic]. That sometime in the fall of the Year, One Thousand Eight Hundred and Fifteen, shortly before Christmas the deponant came past the house of the said Christian Kelheffer, the said Mary [sic] the wife of the said Christian Kelheffer was before the door, and her nose was bloody. She the said Mary [sic] then informed deponant [sic], that her husband, the said Christian had struck her, which was the cause of her bloody nose. Christian was near them, must have heard the complaint, for he was quite near the said Mary [sic], and made no reply, but his appearance was very bad."

Dec. 5, 1820 - Deposition of John Reply "being affirmed according to law saith that he is only particularly acquainted with Christian Kelheffer the Defendant in this suit, that he mearly [sic] knows him by sight, and had very little intercourse with him except what conversation he had with him concerning his wife Mary Kelheffer (formerly Yeiter) [sic] whom he knows and is acquainted with from her infancy. That to the best of his knowledge the said Mary's [sic] character hath always been good and stood fair with her acquaintances. And affirmant further saith that sometime either in the latter part of the year 1815 or the beginning of the year 1816 the said Mary [sic] called at his affirmant's house, and declared that her husband, the said Christian treated her so roughly, that she was in fear of her life to live with him. That he hath latterly [sic] loden [sic] his gun and set the same behind the door and also put a large club with it. And affirmant further saith that the said Mary [sic] prevailed on him to go and speak to the said Christian concerning the circumstances aforesaid, and informed the said Christian that the said Mary [sic] could not live with him under the circumstances of his former conduct towards her and when affirmant came to speak to the said Christian touching the matters aforesaid, he the said Christian made many expressions withing [sic] conversation the most of which affirmant does not recollect, but declared that he would be sharper with her than ever he had been before and requested affirmant to inform the said Mary [sic] of his intentions. Affirmant further saith that he thought proper not to mention the declarations of the said Christian, and persuaded the said Mary [sic] to return to and try to live with him her said husband, and if he scoled [sic] she should say nothing that they might perhaps live together. The said Mary [sic] then left the house and as much as affirmant knows went to and tried to live with her said husband the said Christian, but after sometime affirmant was informed that the said Mary [sic] had separated from her husband the said Christian. And that the said Christian after the said Mary [sic] had left him came to affirmant's house and desired him to go to the said Mary [sic] and ask her if she would not come home again. Affirmant than asked the said Christian if he believed in his heart that they would do well if the said Mary [sic] would go home, the said Christian then replied that he did not think they would do well together. Affirmant then asked the said Christian what his motives were to get the said Mary [sic] home again, if he thought they would not do well together. He the said Christian said that he should not tell the said Mary [sic] to come home, that he should only ask her whether she was not willing to come home. And further saith not."

Cost of depositions was $2.18 including Eshelman's charge for twenty miles, Gallegher's charge for eight miles and Repley's charge for fourteen miles.

Lancaster Co., Pa., Appearance Docket Aug. Term 1817 #275 - Jeremiah Mosher vs. Susan Mosher, libel in divorce.

Aug. 17, 1822 - Court appointed Henry Knowle and Nicholas Hodges to take depositions in this case at Georgetown in the District of Columbia.

Aug. 23, 1822 - Deposition of Mary Hill, colored woman, aged forty years and upwards, of good character, resides in Georgetown District now and for about fifteen years last past. She had known both Jeremiah and Susan Mosher about fifteen years except "last six or seven which time they have been absent from town," "further saith, that she lived in the family with them, a hireling, about eight months constant, and after frequently worked daywork with them, besides often visiting at their house. That during all this time, they the Libellant and Respondent lived as man and wife together, that in the latter part she, the witness, observed several disputing between them, of a jaring nature during which, they spoke German, which the witness did not understand she did not however never see any blows between them." She recalled Sarah leaving her husband several times "of short duration" in 1815 before she left her husband for good. After his wife left, she was sent for to live with and wait on Jeremiah. During that time he was "considerably indisposed" but she felt this was because his wife had left him. Jeremiah left town about three weeks after his wife left him.

Aug. 28, 1822 - Deposition of Capt. Ezra Patterson, of lawful age. He became acquainted with Jeremiah Mosher, Jr., in the year 1805 or 1806 then shortly thereafter met his wife. "Further saith that he the witness lived a neighbor to Mr. Mosher, and was in the habit of frequently calling at his shop where he had considerable work done and that he was frequently in his Mosher's house and never saw anything but harmony and good will between him and his wife." He felt Mr. Mosher was a good husband who treated his wife well.

Aug. 29, 1822 - Deposition of John Libbey, blacksmith, of lawful age. He knew Jeremiah Mosher and Sarah, his wife, about nine or ten years past. He worked as a journeyman blacksmith with Jeremiah Mosher. He was often in the Mosher home and often ate there and never saw or heard "any rangling, or quareling between them." He considered Jeremiah a good husband. His wife left him about seven years ago. Jeremiah "was in a state of bad health, at and before the time Respondent left him, separated from him, and continued sick for a considerable while after." He thought Jeremiah stayed in town three or four months after his wife left him.

Aug. 30, 1822 - Deposition of Dr. William Baker who was the family physician of Mr. and Mrs. Mosher since Mar. 1812, at which time they lived as man and wife in Georgetown, District of Columbia. He felt Jeremiah was a good husband. Jeremiah became infirm in 1814 and 1815 and in 1815 he had "entertained apprehension of his ultimate recovery." He then had fistulous swellings, frequent disorder of the bowels, accompanied with general debility. "He had also threatening of pulmonary disease, which although slow in it's progress, is too often insidious and fatal."

Lancaster Co., Pa., Appearance Docket Nov. Term 1817 #43 - Susan Kesler by her next friend, Thomas Gracious, vs. Andrew Kesler, libel in divorce.

Aug. 15, 1817 - Petition of Susan Kesler (formerly Susan Breniz-er) of the borough of Lancaster, Pa., by her next friend, Thomas Gracious. She married Andrew Kesler in Nov. of 1811 when she was was "upwards of 21 years of age." Andrew Kesler deserted her in Jul. of 1815 while they were living in the borough of Lancaster, Pa. Susan Kesler signed her petition "by mark."

Aug. 30, 1817 - Court issued a subpoena to Andrew Kesler to appear in court to answer the libel of his wife, Susan Kesler, for a divorce.

Lancaster Co., Pa. Appearance Docket Apr. Term 1818 #299 - Susan Kesler by her next friend, Thomas Gracious, vs. Andrew Kesler, libel in divorce.

Mar. 27, 1819 - The court appointed Samuel Dale, Esq., to take depositions. Original documents are now missing.

Lancaster Co., Pa., Appearance Docket Nov. Term 1817 #133 - Sarah Perry by her next friend, Robert Lithgoe, vs. Samuel Perry, libel in divorce.

Oct. 13, 1817 - Petition of Sarah Perry by her next friend, Robert Lithgoe, before John Hoff, justice of the peace. She married Samuel Perry in May of 1808. Samuel Perry deserted her without any just cause in the spring of 1809. Sarah Perry signed her petition "by mark."

Oct. 13, 1817 - Court issued a subpoena to Samuel Perry to appear in court to answer the libel of his wife, Sarah Perry, for a divorce.

Dec. 22, 1817 - Court appointed John Hoff, Esq., to take depositions in this case.

Dec. 23, 1817 - Deposition of Martha Lithgow [sic] who was present at the marriage of Samuel and Sarah Perry. He left her about nine 1years ago and has not lived with her or provided for her since. She added "during the time he did live with her he did not provide for her."

Dec. 23, 1817 - Deposition of Robert Lithgow [sic] - "Robert Lith-gow also appeared before the same Commissioner who upon his oath duly taken saith that Samuel Perry lived at his house with his wife Sarah Perry about seven months and is now about nine years since he the said Samuel left his wife Sarah and hath not lived, main-tained or provided for her in that time. Further saith not."

Lancaster Co., Pa., Appearance Docket Jan. Term 1818 #110 - Sarah Perry by her next friend, Robert Lithgoe, vs. Samuel Perry, libel in divorce. Alias subpoena for Samuel Perry to appear in court to answer the libel of his wife, Sarah Perry, for a divorce.

Apr. 25, 1818 - George Hambright, sheriff of Lancaster Co., Pa., testified he had put notice in the *Lancaster Journal* for four succes-sive weeks. Depositions of Martha Lithgow [sic] and Robert Lithgow [sic] were read to the court and the court granted Sarah Perry a divorce from her husband Samuel Perry. Original documents are now missing.

Lancaster Co., Pa., Appearance Docket Jan. Term 1818 #63 - Sophia Meylin by her next friend, Mary Zehmer, vs. John Meylin, libel in divorce.

Dec. 2, 1817 - Petition of Sophia Meylin by her next friend, Mary Zehmer, that she married John Meylin in Feb. of 1807. He deserted her without any just cause or reason Oct. 2, 1815.

Dec. 2, 1817 - Court issued a subpoena to John Meylin to appear in court to answer the libel of his wife, Sophia Meylin, for a divorce. Contd. to Apr. Term 1818 #43.

Lancaster Co., Pa., Appearance Docket Apr. Term 1818 #68 - Mary Shriver by her next friend, Jacob Sherer, vs. John Shriver, libel for a divorce.

Jan. 23, 1818 - Petition of Mary Shriver by her next friend, Jacob Sherer, now of the borough of Lancaster, Pa. She married July 9, 1807, John Shriver of Adams Co., Pa. "That about five or six years past he became subject to drunkeness [sic] and in consequence thereof subject to frequent derangment [sic] and subjected her frequently to the danger of losing her life from his cruelty and going constantly around with a loaded gun threatening to destroy her, thereby keeping her in constant fear. That from his habits of intoxication, his property was squandered and she from that cirumstance, and his cruelty, was obliged to abandon him in order to provide a subsistance [sic] for herself and her children, and that since her separating she is informed that he has contracted matrimony with another woman and is now living in a state of adultery with him."

Jan. 26, 1818 - Court issued a subpoena to John Shriver to appear in court to answer the libel of his wife, Mary Shriver, for a divorce.

Lancaster Co., Pa., Appearance Docket Aug. Term 1818 #109 - Mary Shriver by her next friend, Jacob Sherer, vs. John Shriver, libel in divorce.

Aug. 19, 1818 - Court appointed George Nace of Hanover, York Co., Pa., to take depositions in this case.

Nov. 20, 1818 - "Samuel Carpenter personally appeared in open court and he being solemnly affirmed - sayeth that his daughter Mary Carpenter now Mary Shriver the complainant was lawfully married by the Reverand [sic] Henry Hoffmyer on the 9th day of July 1807 to the Defendant John Shriver of Adams County - and that she lived with him as his wife until the latter end of March 1815 when she was obliged to leave him in consequence of his deranged state of mind, arising out of continual intoxication, and the danger arising therefrom of loss of life - which he verily believes to be true - and further sayeth not. Affirmed in open court the 20th of November

1818. Attest." Signed by G. B. Porter, Prothy., and Saml. Carpenter.

Nov. 14, 1818 - "Interrogations to be administered to witnesses for and on behalf of the Complainant. #1 Do you know the parties in this cause and how long have you known them. Declare. #2 Do you know at what time they were married, when, where, and by whom - and how long they lived together in a married state. #3 Do you know of any bad treatment shown by defendant to complainant - if yea - declare your knowledge thereof fully and at large. #4 Do you know of defendant's having lately intermarried with another woman - If yea - declare your knowledge thereof, fully and at large, her name, when, where and by whom they were married. Last Do you know of any other matter or thing beneficial to complainant - if yea - declare your knowledge thereof fully and at large. Nov. 14th 1818." Signed by W. P. Frazer, solicitor for libellant.

Nov. 18, 1818 - "County of York, Pa. Seal - Before David Shultz, Esquire, one of the Justice of the Peace in and for said County and George Nace, Commissioner named in the within Rule - personally appeared the Revd. John Herbst of Manchester (Maryland) who upon his solemn oath according to law marks the following answers to the interrogations filed in the said Rule viz: To 1st Interrogatory Deponent answers that he does not know the parties. To 2nd Interrogatory Deponent answers that he does not know at what time the parties were married neither when, where or by whom and that he does not know how long they lived together in a married state. To 3rd Interrogatory Deponant [sic] also says that he knows of no bad treatment as he did not know the parties. To 4th Interrogatory Deponant [sic] answers that about 15 months ago a certain John Shriver and Flory Spealman accompanied by the father of said Flory, came to his house in Manchester aforesaid, and desired him (the Deponent) to marry them, that deponent asked them for a license and that they had none, that he the deponant [sic] then published the bans in open church and in the afternoon of said day married them. To 5th Interrogatory Deponant [sic] answers that he knows of nothing else that in his opinion would have given benefit to the complaintant [sic]. Sworn and subscribed the Eighteenth day of November A.D. 1818 Before" Signed by David Smith, justice, Geo. Nace, commissioner, and Rev. John Herbst (who signed in German script).

Nov. 16, 1818 - "County of York, Pa. Seal - In pursuance of the foregoing rule appeared before David Shultz, Esquire, one of the Justices of the Peace in and for said county in the presances [sic] of George Nace, Commissioner within named George Eckert and David Eckert both of the County of Adams who being duly sworn according to law for their solemn oaths do say and declare as follows. To first interrogatory the deponents do both say that they knew the defendant for upwards of ten years and the complainant [sic] for about seven or eight years. To the second interrogatory Deponents answer that they do not know at what time the parties were married or where or by whom, but that they know they have lived together as man and wife for four or five years. To third interrogatory Deponants [sic] answers that they know of no maltreatment of the defendant towards the complaintant, but that the defendant has been frequently drunk. To fourth interrogatory Deponants [sic] say that the defendant acknowledged to them that he (the Defendant) had been married to a certain Flory Spealman, that they were married at Manchester (Maryland) by the Reverend Mr. Herbst, and that the said defendant had also acknowledged that he had a son by the said Flory Spealman. To fifth interrogatory deponants [sic] say that they know of nothing else that in their opinion could or might be of benefit to complaint. Sworn and subscribed the 16th day of November A.D. 1818 Before" Signed by David Shultz, justice, Geo. Nace, commissioner, George Eckert, and David Eckert.

Nov. 20, 1818 - Deposition of Samuel Carpenter, Esq., and others were read to the court and the court granted Mary Shriver a divorce from her husband, John Shriver.

Lancaster Co., Pa., Appearance Docket Apr. Term 1818 #100 - Mary Kline by her next friend, John Lind, vs. John Kline, libel in divorce.

Feb. 18, 1818 - Petition of Mary Kline hy her next friend, John Lind, before Walter Franklin. She married John Kline Sept. 17, 1809. He abused her and endangered her life causing her to leave him. Mary Kline signed her petition "by mark."

Feb. 18, 1818 - Court issued a subpoena to John Kline to appear in court to answer the libel of his wife, Mary Kline, for a divorce.

Apr. 21, 1818 - "On motion of Mr. Hopkins, the Court appoints Samuel Carpenter, Esq. Commissioner to take the examination of witnesses in the case of Mary Kline the libellant - Attest for George B. Porter, Prothy." Signed by Jno. Hall.

Apr. 23, 1818 - "In pursuance of the above rule, personally came before me Samuel Carpenter, one of the Justices of the Peace in and for the said County of Lancaster, and Commissioner in the above rule named, Elizabeth Mawer of Manheim Township, the wife of Henry Mawer, who being duly sworn according to law, deposeth and says, that John Klein and Mary his wife, about six or seven years ago, lived in her father's house, situate [sic] in the Borough of Lancaster, where she this deponant [sic] lived at home with her and father, Andrew Luby, and that the said Klein and his said wife, frequently quarreled, and led a disagreeable life, but never saw the said Klein beat his wife, neither doth this deponant [sic] know who was the cause of their quarreling, whether it was the husband or wife, but one time she recolected [sic] that they the said Klein and his wife were heard quarreling, for some lenth [sic] of time, but what was said between them, this deponant [sic] could not understand, but says that after the quarrel last mentioned ceased they appeared to be quite silent, and not a word heard from them, the people in the house with her this deponant [sic], began to feel alarmed, dreading some evil consequences, and some of them attempted to enter the apartment, where the said Klein and his wife were in, but found the door as well as the window shutters fastened, so that they could not enter as aforesaid, they then concluded to send forth the said Klein's father as well as his father-in-law, which they accordingly did, and when they came, they got the window shutter open and same went in through the window then the door was opened but by whom, this deponant [sic] could not say, and when she this deponant [sic] entered the room, she the said Mary Klein apparantly lay lifeless on the floor and the said Klein was setting on a chair as in a sleep and that the said Klein got drunk very frequently while living at the place aforesaid, once and when so drunk as aforesaid the quarreling generally commenced. And further saith not. Sworn and subscribed the 23 day of Apr. 1818 before me." Signed by Saml. Carpenter and Elizabeth Mawer.

Apr. 23, 1818 - "Elizabeth Leibly sworn, says, that about six or seven years ago, John Klein and Mary his wife, had rented half of her house wherein this deponant [sic] herself with her family resided at the same time, and that during the time that said Klein and his wife lived with them this deponant [sic] and family in the same house as aforesaid, the said John Klein very frequently got to be intoxicated, and when so, he was quarrelsome and abusive to his said wife, when generally quarrels between them ensued, but as the said Klein and his wife lived in a seperate [sic] appartment [sic] of the said house, this deponant only heard and did not see their squabbles, and therefore never saw this said Klein beat his wife. This deponant [sic] further saith that one evening when she and her family were at supper, they heard a noise and a scuffle in the appartment [sic] wherein said Klein and his wife resided as aforesaid and that the door was locked in as immediately after the scuffell [sic] dangerous consequences were feared, and when an attempt was main to enter the said Klein's appartment [sic] the door was found to be locked, and that the door was then opened, how this deponant [sic] doth not recolect [sic], nor who opened the same, but when she entered the room the said Mary Klein, the wife of the same John Klein, was laying on the floor, apparently lifeless, and the said Klein was sitting on a chair near the stove apparently drunk, but what happened or how the said Mary became to lay as aforesaid, she could not say. And this deponant further saith that as much as she knows, and verily believeth, the said Klein at that time provided sufficiently for his family, at least in so much that they did not want. And further saith not. Sworn and subscribed the 23 day of April 1818 before me." Signed by Saml. Carpenter and Elizabeth Liebly by "her mark."

Apr. 29, 1818 - "Thomas Michan being duly sworn according to Law deposeth and says, that he served an apprenticeship with John Klein and lived with him the said Klein, and Mary his wife, for upwards (of) six years, and that during that time, the said John Klein was intoxicated, the most of his time and very seldom remained sober for a whole day, and that when he was intoxicated he was very abusive to his said wife Mary, and quarreled with and ill treated his said wife, almost every day during that time, and that he one time saw the said John Klein throw a brick bat or stone (he is not sure which, but believes it was a brick bat) at and hit his wife therewith to one of her legs, by which she appeared to be much hurted [sic], and that, that was the only time he saw the said Klein hurt his wife, by with striking or throwing at and hiting [sic] her, but that he very frequently heard the said Klein threatening to beat her his said wife, and making use of threatening and terrifying language, (as is meant by the inpression [sic] above stated abusive and ill treated). And this deponant [sic] further saith, that during the time he lived with the said Klein as aforesaid, it appeared to him, that the treatment that Mary the wife of the said John Klein, received from her husband the said John Klein, must have made her condition intolerable and her life birthensome[sic]. And this deponant [sic] further says that he recoleets [sic] that during the time of his apprecticeship he the said John Klein one evening put his said wife Mary out of the house, locked the door on her, and kept her out all that night. And this deponant [sic] further saith that during his apprenticeship aforesaid, the said Mary the wife of the said John Klein, behaved herself towards her said husband as him this deponant [sic] believes, as a good wife and mistress. And this deponant [sic] further saith, that his said Master the said John Klein which was his apprecticer, ordered him to beat his said Mistress, the wife of the said Klein, which he refused to do. And further saith not. Sworn and subscribed the 29th day April 1818." Signed by Saml. Carpenter and Thom. Mighten [sic].

Apr. 21, 1818 - "April 21st, 1818 - On motion of Mr. Hopkins, the Court appoint(s) William Wilkinson, Esq., Commissioner to take the examination of witnesses, in the case of Mary Kline the libellant. Attest for George B. Porter, Prothy." Signed by Jno. Hall.

Apr. 25, 1818 - "In pursuance of the above Commission I have this day examined and taken the depositions of the following persons viz. Jacob Wallick, Peter Histan, James Galbraeth, Doct. John Watson, Esther Mayers, Annah Heston, and John Sheller, as will appear by the schedule here to answer. In witness where I have hereto set my hand and seal at morning of the 25th day of Apr. A.D. 1818. Justice costs were $1.93, court costs were $2.05, and Witnesses cost was $2.10 making a total cost of $6.18." Signed by William Wilkinson.

Apr. 25, 1818 - "Jacob Wallick of the Township of Repho in the County of Lancaster being produced affirmed and examined on behalf of the plaintiff in the title of the above Commission. Doth depose and say as follows. That he has heard them the said Mary Kline and John Kline scolding and I heard the said John Kline say frequently that he would thrash or whip her if she would not hold her Toung [sic] and further saith not. Affirmed and subscribed before me April 25th 1818." Signed by Wm. Wilkinson and Jacob Wallick.

Apr. 25, 1818 - "Peter Hestan of the Township of Mout [sic] Joy in the County of Lancaster being produced and affirmed and examined as above, doth depose and say as follows. That the said Mary Kline came to his house one night or evening and requested him and his wife to go with her the said Mary Kline to her house which they did and he the said deponent requested the said John Kline to let her in which he the said John Kline refused to do. That the said Mary Kline then went back with them and staid [sic] that night and further that he this deponent frequently saw the said John Kline intoxicated which he belieaves [sic] to have been the case at that time when he refused her admittance and further saith not. Affirmed and subscribed before me April 25th 1818." Signed by Wm. Wilkinson and Peter Hestan.

Apr. 25, 1818 - "James Galbraith of the Town of Mout [sic] Joy in the County of Lancaster being produced and sworn and examined as above. Doth depose and say as follows. That he the said John Kline was very frequently intoxicated and did not appear to him to pay that attention to his family that a man ought to do but concearning [sic] any harsh treatment that the said John Kline gave her other wise [sic] he says he knows not. Sworn and subscribed before me April 25th 1818." Signed by Wm. Wilkinson and James Galbraith.

Apr. 25, 1818 - "Doctor John Watson of the Township of Donogall in the County of Lancaster being produced sworn and examined on behalf of Plaintiff in the title of the above Commission who deposeth and saith that during the months of July, August, September and October he attended John Kline's leg and that the said Mary Kline seamed [sic] to pay every attention that a wife ought to, to him the said John Kline and further saith not. Sworn and subscribed before me Apr. 25th 1818." Signed by John Watson.

Apr. 25, 1818 - "Esther Myers of the Township of Mount Joy in the County of Lancaster being produced and affirmed and examined as above mentioned doth depose and say as follows. That she has herd [sic] John Kline threaten to whip her. That he would take the cowskin and cowskin her the said Mary Kline his wife and that on or about the night of the 24th of January last the said Mary Kline came to their house at a late hour and said that the said John Kline was at the Tavern and that she was afraid to go to bed for he would come home drunk and make her get up again and requested this deponent to let her girl go over with her awhile which she consented to. Some short time after the girl came over and told this deponent to come over to Kline's for God sake that Kline had threatened that he would massacre her the said Mary Kline. Then this deponent [sic] went over and found the said Mary standing at the beaura [sic] crying and enquiring the matter the said John Kline made answer and said O that damned fool. She the said Mary asked the said John if she might have half the goods if she would go. He said yes and go as soon as God will let you and further saith not. Affirmed and subscribed before me April 25th 1818." Signed by Wm. Wilkinson and Esther Myers.

Apr. 25, 1818 - "Anna Hestan of the Township of Mount Joy in the County of Lancaster being produced affirmed and examined on behalf of the above Commission doth depose and say as follows. That the said Mary Kline came to her house in the evening of one night (the time not recollected) and told that the said John Kline had fastened her out of the house and request Peter Hestan and herself, this deponent [sic] to go along with her to his house which they did and he the said John Kline refused to let her in the house and that she the said Mary Kline then wint [sic] along with them to their house and staid [sic] that night, and further she saith she knoweth not. Affirmed and subscribed before me April 25th 1818." Signed by Wm. Wilkinson and Anna Hestan by "her mark."

Apr. 25, 1818 - "John Sheller of the Township of Mount Joy in the County of Lancaster being produced affirmed and examined on behalf of the plaintiff in the title of the above Commission doth depose and say as follows. That he has frequently heard John Kline abuse his wife Mary Kline mistreating her and it appeared to him without any provication [sic] and that he has heard the said John Kline say about eight or ten days ago or their abouts that he did not wish to live with her any more. If he could be with her one night she might go to the Devil then and further saith not. Affirmed and subscribed before me April 25th 1818." Signed by Wm. Wilkinson and John Sheller.

Apr. 30, 1818 - Depositions of Elizabeth Mawer and others read to the court and the court granted Mary Kline a divorce from her husband, John Kline. Total cost was $12.37.

Lancaster Co., Pa., Appearance Docket Apr. Term 1818 #164 - Susan Forney by her next friend, Philip Roth, vs. Abraham Forney, Jr., libel in divorce.

Mar. 9, 1818 - Petition of Susan Forney by her next friend, Philip Roth, stated that she married on May 5, 1816, Abraham Forney, Jr., of Cocalico Twp., Lancaster Co., Pa. On Apr. 21, 1817, "she was driven by force and violance [*sic*] of her said husband from his dwelling and when she was compelled to seek an asylum (in order to save her life) in the house of her father and that his abuse of her previous to that time was so great that she was in constant fear and apprehension of the loss of life."

Apr. 27, 1818 - "on motion of Mr. Frazer, leave granted to withdraw the petition or libel for divorce."

Jun. 3, 1818 - "petition and affidavit taken out of the office by Mr. Frazer."

Lancaster Co., Pa., Appearance Docket Aug. Term 1818 #130 - Ann Getz by her next friend, Henry Neff, vs. Joseph Getz, libel in divorce.

Jun. 1, 1818 - Petition of Ann Getz, wife of Joseph Getz, late of Hempfield Twp., Lancaster Co., Pa., by her next friend, Henry Neff. She married about eleven years ago Joseph Getz and lived with him between seven and eight years. "During which period she experienced very hard treatment from the said Joseph and that upwards of three years ago, the said Joseph entirely abandoned and deserted your petitioner and has gone to places unknown to your petitioner." Ann Getz signed her petition "by mark."

Aug. 22, 1818 - The court appointed John Hoff, Esq., to take depositions in this case and on Oct. 5, 1818, the court replaced him with John Light, Esq.

Lancaster Co., Pa., Appearance Docket Nov. Term 1818 #35 - Ann Getz by her next friend, Henry Neff, vs. Joseph Getz, libel in divorce.

Oct. 3, 1818 - Court appointed John Light, Esq., to take depositions in this case.

Oct. 7, 1818 - Deposition of Henry Bear of Hempfield Twp., Lancaster Co., Pa. - who knew Joseph and Ann Getz. "That he understood by report only that the said Joseph Getz was unkind in his behavior towards the said Ann and rendered her life uncomfortable. That about four years ago, the said Joseph Getz left his wife and, has ever since totally deserted and abandoned her the said Ann his wife the libellant in this case. Nor has he ever since cohabited with her. Nor does this affirmant know where the said Joseph Getz the defendant now is. But he has heard that he went to Philadelphia, where he listed [*sic*] and went to sea and further this affirmant knoweth not." Signed by Henry Bear.

Oct. 7, 1818 - Deposition of John Rupley of the city of Lancaster. "He well knows that the said Joseph's behavior toward the said Ann was abusive and unbecoming a husband, so as to render her life uncomfortable. That nearly four years past, the said Joseph Getz, left his said wife, and as this affirmant verily believes, never since cohabited with the said Ann, but totally deserted her, and left her to maintain herself." Signed by John Rupley.

Jan. 18, 1819 - Depositions of Henry Bear and John Rupley read to the court and the court granted Ann Getz a divorce from her husband, Joseph Getz.

Lancaster Co., Pa., Appearance Docket Aug. Term 1818 #158 - Susan Forney by her next friend, John Roth, vs. Abraham Forney, Jr., libel in divorce.

Jun. 3, 1818 - Petition of Susan Forney before Samuel Carpenter. She married Abraham Forney, Jr., of Earl Twp., Lancaster Co., Pa., on May 5, 1816. She was driven by force from his dwelling and compelled to "fly" to the house of her father to save her life on Apr. 21 or 22 of 1817.

Aug. 19, 1818 - Court appointed Samuel Carpenter, Esq., to take depositions in this case at 10 o'clock A.M. on Aug. 26, 1818.

Aug. 20, 1818 - Rule on defendant to file his answer on or before the first day of next term and a rule to take depositions at any time on three days notice to the defendant

Aug. 26, 1818 - "And now August 1818 Rule at the Instance of Plaintiff's attorney that depositions to be read in evidence on the trial of this cause be taken before Saml. Carpenter, Esq. a Justice of the Peace at his office in the City of Lancaster on Wednesday the 26th August 1818 at 10 o'clock A.M. Exparte Rule on 3 days notice. Attest. G. B. Porter, Prothy."

Aug. 26, 1818 - "City of Lancaster - Samuel Michael sworn according to law deposeth and saith, that some time in the spring of the year 1817 (if deponant [sic] recolects [sic] right it was in the month of April) he lived about two days with Abm. Forney, Jun. [sic] who at that time lived in Warwick Township, and who is defendant in this cause, that at that time the said Abm. Forney was sick, or at least pretended to be so, and that the said Forney during the time he lived with him, the few days aforesaid, was almost continually quarreling with his wife, the Plaintiff in this case, and seen him the said Forney make a push at his said wife with his hand, and heard him threaten to throw the Chamber bed at her and deponant [sic] further saith, that at one time the said Forney accused his said wife in deponant's [sic] presents [sic], of whouring [sic] with him, the deponant [sic], and deponant [sic] furhter [sic] saith that the conduct of the said Forney towards his said wife while he deponant [sic] lived with him the few days aforesaid was such as to make her living with him intolerable and her life burdensome, that he forbid his said wife to sleep in the same Chamber with him, and desired the maid to sleep in his bed chamber, which the maid refused to do. Justice by Deft. - Do you not know or recolect [sic] that I could not help myself at that time, that I was to be lifted about in my bed? Answer - I know no further than that I myself helped lift you several times to turn, etc., in bed, and further saith not. Sworn, subscribed and examined before me the Justice in the foregoing rule named in the presence of the Defendant Abm. Forney, Jun. the 26th day of August

1818." Signed by Saml. Carpenter and Samuel Michael by "his mark."

Aug. 26, 1818 - "City of Lancaster - Mary Miller sworn according to law deposeth and saith, that in the spring of the year 1817 she lived with Abrm. [sic] Forney, Jun. [sic] as a Hirling for the space of between three and four weeks. That the said Forney was sick or pretended to be sick almost the whole of that time, excepting a few days in the beginning of that time, and that during that time, the said Forney treated his wife very ill, such as cutting and quarreling with her, and forbid his said wife (the plaintiff in this cause) to come into his sick chamber, and several times threatened to beat her, and followed her in a threatening manner, calling her Chimney sweep and a damned whore, and that the said Forney desired Defendant to sleep in the same chamber with him, after forbiding his wife to enter the same, which Deponant [sic] refused to do, and his wife was not allowed to come neer [sic] him, and provide any victuals for him. And deponant [sic] further saith, that the wife of the said Forney paid all the required attention to her said husband, as long as she was permited [sic] so to do, and fretted much concerning the usuage she received from her husband as aforesaid. And deponant [sic] further that the said Forney one time chased his wife downstairs in such a fright and hurry, he pursuing her she stumbled down all the steps at one time. And deponant [sic] further saith that one night when she and the wife of the said Forney were setting in the kitchen that said Forney swore several times out, in the kitchen aforesaid, calling his wife bad names, amongst them a whore and when he came the third time he attempted to beat his said wife, when she made his escape and left the house, and did not return that night, and that after the escape of his wife aforesaid, the said Forney went on cursing and swearing in such a manner as frightened deponant [sic], that she also left the house the same night, and did not return to live with the said Forney again, neither did his wife return to her husband since that time, to her knowledge. Question by Defendant - What did my wife say when I came to the kitchen at the time when you say I chased my wife out? Answer - She called you a Damned Ram. Jury by the same - Did you never see that I was so weak as to be lifted about in my bed? Answer - Yes, I have seen that they lifted you about and was informed that people sat up with you all night for a few nights only. And further saith not. Sworn to and subscribed before me the Justice of the Peace in the foregoing rule named in the presence of Defendant the 26th day of August 1818." Signed by Saml. Carpenter and Mary Miller by "her mark."

Aug. 26, 1818 - "Adjourned to one o'clock in the afternoon of the same day parties, plaintiff being represented by her father Philip Roth and councel [sic] William C. Sharer, Esq. Defendant presant [sic]. - City of Lancaster - Philip Roth being duly affirmed according to law declares and saith, that Susanna Forney the wife of Abrm.

[sic] Forney, Jun. [sic], the plaintiff in this case, she being a daughter of affirmant, was under the necessity of leaving her said husband's house as well as bed and board, in consequence of ill treatment she received from her said husband - and further saith not. Affirmed and subscribed the 26th day of August in the presence of Defendant before me the Justice in the foregoing rule named." Signed by Saml. Carpenter and Philip Roth (who signed in German script).

Oct. 5, 1818 - William Hopkins, atty. for defendant, comes into court and for answer says the allegations of plaintiff are unfounded and prays an issue which is accordingly granted.

Lancaster Co., Pa., Appearance Docket Nov. Term 1818 #33 - Sophia Albright by her next friend, Robert Wilson, vs. Peter Albright, libel in divorce.

Aug. 3, 1818 - Petition of Sophia Albright by her next friend, Robert Wilson, stated that she married in 1810 Peter Albright. Her husband deserted her upwards of two years ago without any just cause.

Lancaster Co., Pa., Appearance Docket Jan. Term 1819 #20 - Sophia Albright by her next friend, Robert Wilson, vs. Peter Albright, libel in divorce.

Jan. 21, 1819 - Court appointed William B. Ross to take depositions in this case.

Apr. 13, 1819 - Deposition of Peter Hawman that "the said Peter willfully and maliciously deserted his said wife without any reasonable cause for the space of two years and upwards previous to the filing the libel in the above cause and to the best of his knowledge and belief has never cohabited with or provided anything for her and her child during the said period or since."

Apr. 13, 1819 - Deposition of Robert Wilson before John Light who "doth depose and say that the above named Sophia is his daughter and that she was joined in lawful matrimony with said Peter Albright and during the time of their cohabitation she bore him two children of whom one is yet living and that the said Peter has been guilty of great cruelty abuse and most barbarous conduct to his said wife.

Apr. 10, 1819 - Deposition of John Ruply before John Light who "doth declare and say that has been acquainted with the parties to the above suit for some years past and that the said Sophia Albright has resided in the neighborhood where this affirmant lives for two or three years and has one child. And that the said Peter willfully and maliciously deserted his wife without any reasonable cause for two years and upwards and previous to the filing the libel in the above cause and belief [sic] has never since lived with his wife or provided for her or her child and further saith not."

Apr. 19, 1819 - Depositions of Peter Hawman, John Ruply, and

Robert Wilson were read to the court and the court granted Sophia Albright a divorce from her husband, Peter Albright. Cost of divorce was $12.50.

Lancaster Co., Pa., Appearance Docket Nov. Term 1818 #34 - Mary Arthur by her next friend, William Baker, vs. Robert Arthur, libel in divorce.

Jun. 15, 1818 - Petition of Mary Arthur by her next friend, William Baker, stated that she married Robert Arthur on Jan. 17, 1811. He abused her and endangered her life and she was forced to leave him in Apr. of 1818.

Aug. 17, 1818 - Court issued a subpoena to Robert Arthur to appear in court to answer the libel of his wife, Mary Arthur, for a divorce.

Nov. 14, 1818 - Robert Arthur answers the libel of his wife and admits the marriage date but "doth expressly deny the charge of cruel and barbarous treatment so as to endanger the life of the said Mary Arthur the libellant or of offering such indignities to her person as to render her condition intolerable or her life burdensome and thereby forced her to withdraw from the defendant's house and family." Affidavit filed. Costs were $7.75. "Ende [sic] says William Holliday brother-in-law of Mary Arthur."

Lancaster Co., Pa., Appearance Docket Nov. Term 1818 #120 - Phoebe Lowmase by her next friend, Eli H. Thomas, vs. James Lowmase, libel in divorce.

Oct. 5, 1818 - Petition of Phoebe H. Lowmase by her next friend, Eli H. Thomas, stated she married James Lowmase on or about Dec. 17, 1815. He willfully deserted her two years past and upwards. She also testified that she is a native of Pa., and has always lived there.

Lancaster Co., Pa., Appearance Docket Jan. Term 1819 #75 - Phoebe Lawmase by her next friend, Eli H. Thomas, vs. James Lowmase, libel in divorce.

Jan. 21, 1819 - The court appointed John Light, Esq., to take depositions in this case.

Jan. 27, 1819 - Deposition of "John Forney of the City of Lancaster and Christiana Forney his wife who upon oath say that James Lomax [sic] went off and left his wife Phebe [sic] sometime in the month of October A.D. 1816. Shortly after James Lomax [sic] left Lancaster these deponants [sic] heard that he was in Baltimore, but have heard nothing from him since, that they have not seen him nor heard of his being in these parts since he left here in 1816. These deponants [sic] further say that they have not heard of any support being formed or given by the said James Lomax [sic] for the maintence [sic] of his said wife and further say not." John Forney signed his deposition and his wife, Christiana Forney, signed "by mark."

Jan. 28, 1819 - Deposition of Dr. Abraham Carpenter, of the city of Lancaster, who "doth declare and say that in the autumn of 1816 he attended Mrs. Lomax [sic], wife of James Lomax [sic], in her lying in and before that time that her husband had then left her in great distress and left no provision for her. That this affirmant hath not seen him since and is confident that the said James Lomax [sic] hath not been in these parts since nor contributed anything towards the maintence [sic] of Phebe [sic] Lomax [sic] his wife and further saith not."

Apr. 26, 1819 - Deposition of Amelia Thomas, of Columbia, before John Light. She "doth declare and say, that James Lomax [sic] left his wife Phebe [sic] on the fifth day of September in the year 1816. That he left his wife without any support and in great distress. That he the said James Lomax [sic] hath not been in these parts since. That she can not tel [sic] where he is but knows that he has not provided nor given any support to his wife since he left her."

Apr. 27, 1819 - Depositions of Jacob Forney, Christiana Forney, Dr. Abraham Carpenter, and Amelia Thomas were read to the court. Court granted Phoebe Lowmase a divorce from her husband, James Lomase [sic].

Lancaster Co., Pa., Appearance Docket Nov. Term 1818 #134 - Catharine Lambert by her father and next friend, John Keller, vs. John Lambert, libel in divorce.

Oct. 14, 1818 - Petition of Catharine Lambert by her father and next friend, John Keller. She married about seventeen years ago John Lambert who deserted her about nine years ago. She signed her petition "by mark."

Oct. 14, 1818 - Court issued a subpoena to John Lambert to appear in court to answer the libel of his wife, Catharine Lambert, for a divorce. It was served personally by George Hambright, sheriff

Nov. 18, 1818 - Court appointed John Light, Esq., to take depositions in this case.

Nov. 25, 1818 - Deposition of John Keller before John Light, Esq. "He knows that the said John Lambert was unkind in his behavior to his wife and rendered her life uncomfortable. That about nine years ago the said John left his said wife and has ever since totally deserted and abandoned the said Catharine his wife the Libellant in this case nor has he ever since cohabited with her and that he understands that the said Defendant lives in Lancaster and further this deponent knoweth not."

Nov. 25, 1818 - Deposition of Catharine Bartle before John Light, Esq., who "doth declare and say that she was acquainted with the said John Lambert and Catharine his wife. That she knows the said John's conduct was disorderly by that she has lived in the neighborhood for seven years and knows that during that time he has totally abandoned her and left her to be maintained by her father and further saith not." Catharine Bartle signed "by mark."

Nov. 28, 1818 - Depositions of John Keller and Catharine Bartle were read to the court and the court granted Catharine Lambert a divorce from her husband, John Lambert. Cost was $11.00.

Lancaster Co., Pa., Appearance Docket Jan. Term 1819 #73 - Barbara Goss by her father and next friend, Jacob Miller, vs. John Goss, libel in divorce.

Dec. 2, 1818 - Petition of Barbara Goss by her father and next friend, Jacob Miller, before George Matter. She stated that she married John Goss about three years ago. He abused her and endangered her life thereby forcing her to leave him. Barbara Goss signed her petition "by mark."

Lancaster Co., Pa., Appearance Docket Apr. Term 1819 #50 - Barbara Goss by her father and next friend, Jacob Miller, vs. John Goss, libel in divorce. Original documents in this file are now missing.

Lancaster Co., Pa., Appearance Docket Jan. Term 1819 #74 - William Downey vs. Leanora Downey, libel in divorce.

Dec. 7, 1818 - Petition of William Downey before Samuel Carpenter, justice of the peace. He married Leanora Rawlins in 1815. She deserted him "upwards of two years past" without any reasonable cause.

Dec. 14, 1818 - The court issued a subpoena to Leanora Downey to appear in court to answer the libel of her husband, William Downey, for a divorce.

Lancaster Co., Pa., Appearance Docket Apr. Term 1819 #20 - William Downey vs. Leanora Downey, libel in divorce. Sheriff returns that Leanora Downey was not found in his bailiwick.

Jan. 29, 1819 - Court appointed John S. Andrews, Esq., of the city of Baltimore, Md., to take depositions in this case. Original documents are now missing in this file.

Lancaster Co., Pa., Appearance Docket Jan. Term 1819 #82 - Elizabeth Saunders by her next friend, John Block, vs. Edward Saunders, libel in divorce.

Dec. 17, 1818 - Petition of Elizabeth Saunders by her next friend, John Block, before John Eberman. She stated that she married Edward Saunders May 16, 1814, and he deserted her "two years and upwards" without any just or reasonable cause.

Dec. 17, 1818 - Court issued a subpoena for Edward Saunders to appear in court to answer the libel of his wife, Elizabeth Saunders, for a divorce.

Lancaster Co., Pa., Appearance Docket Apr. Term 1819 #13 - Elizabeth Saunders by her next friend, John Black, vs. Edward Saunders, libel in divorce.

Apr. 30, 1819 - Court appointed John Light, Esq., to take depositions in this case.

Jan. 16, 1823 - "Ended says Plaintiff's attorney Jan. 16, 1823."
Original documents are now missing in this file.

Lancaster Co., Pa., Appearance Docket Aug. Term 1819 #17 -
Anna Kaufman by her nearest friend, Samuel Weidler, vs. Christian
Kaufman, libel in divorce.

Apr. 1, 1819 - Petition of Anna Kaufman by her nearest friend,
Samuel Weidler, that she married about Dec. of 1807 Christian
Kaufman. They lived together five years but he abused her and
made her life a burden. In Jul. of 1813 she left him because his
treatment "of her was inhuman and brutal." He didn't provide for
her. Two years ago he enlisted in the "United Service" and she has
heard from him only once since then. She therefore wants a divorce.
Testified before Samuel Carpenter, Lancaster Co., justice of the
peace. Anna Kaufman signed her petition "by mark."

Apr. 22, 1819 - Petition filed and the court issued a subpoena for
Christian Kaufman to appear in court to answer the libel of his wife
for a divorce.

Lancaster Co., Pa., Appearance Docket Nov. Term 1819 #356 -
Anna Kaufman by her next friend, Samuel Weidler, vs. Christian
Kaufman, libel in divorce.

Jan. 24, 1820 - Court appointed Samuel Carpenter, Esq., to take
depositions in this case.

Apr. 21, 1820 - Depositions of John Breg, Daniel Ehler, Jacob
Frankford, and John Grimes were read to the court. The court then
granted Anna Kaufman a divorce from her husband, Christian
Kaufman. Original documents, which include those four depositions, are now missing from the files.

Lancaster Co., Pa., Appearance Docket Aug. Term #128 - Juliana
Leiblin by her next friend, Robert Barber, vs. Mathias Leiblin, libel in
divorce.

May 19, 1819 - Petition of Juliana Leiblin by her next friend,
Robert Barber. She married Matthias Leiblin in 1808. Her husband
"at divers times hath by cruel and barbarous treatment, endangered
the life of your petitioners, as to render her condition intolerable and
life burthensome [sic], and thereby forced her to withdraw from his
house and family." She therefore left her husband in Mar. of 1818.
She testified this before John Eberman, justice of the peace of
Lancaster Co., Pa.

Jun. 1, 1819 - Petition was filed and the court issued a subpoena
to Mathias Leiblin to appear in court to answer the libel of his wife
Juliana Leiblin for a divorce. Subpoena was served by copy.

Lancaster Co., Pa., Appearance Docket Nov. Term 1819 #36 - Catharine Stickel by her next friend, Daniel Neff, vs. Henry Stickel, libel in divorce.

Aug. 25, 1819 - Petition of Catharine Stickel by her next friend, Daniel Neff. She married Jul. 21, 1815, Henry Stickel and he willfully deserted her three months later without any just or reasonable cause. The date he deserted her was Aug. 14, 1815. Catharine Stickel signed her petition "by mark."

Aug. 25, 1819 - Court issued a subpoena to Henry Stickel to appear in court to answer the libel of his wife, Catharine Stickel, for a divorce.

Lancaster Co., Pa., Appearance Docket Jan. Term 1820 #50 - Catharine Stickel by her next friend, Daniel Neff, vs. Henry Stickel, libel in divorce. Original documents are now missing from this file.

Lancaster Co., Pa., Appearance Docket Nov. Term 1819 #194 - Sarah Black by her next friend, Ann Connelly, vs. Robert Black, libel in divorce.

Oct. 4, 1819 - Petition of Sarah Black by her next friend, Ann Connelly, stated that she married Robert Black on Jun. 1, 1815. Robert Black entered into a second marriage on Jun. 27, 1815, and then willfully deserted her on Sept. 1, 1815, or thereabouts. Sarah Black signed her petition "by mark."

Lancaster Co., Pa., Appearance Docket Jan. Term 1820 #40 - Sarah Black by her next friend, Ann Connelly, vs. Robert Black, libel in divorce.

Apr. 17, 1820 - Court appointed John Passmore, Esq., to take depositions in this case.

Apr. 19, 1820 - Deposition of Charles Connelly who testified that Robert Black married his present wife, Sarah, but about five years ago he absconded from the neighborhood for the charge of having made bad notes. He thinks it was around the time of husking corn that he went away. He left his wife with no provision and has not been seen in the neighborhood since.

Apr. 20, 1820 - Henry Hoffmeur, the present clergyman of the German Reformed Congregation in the City of Lancaster. He testified that he married on Jun. 1, 1815, Robert Black to Sarah Connelly, both of Lampeter Twp., Lancaster Co., Pa.

Apr. 20, 1820 - Deposition of George Matter, justice of the peace of Lancaster Co., Pa., who testified that Robert Black was brought before him on a charge of Elizabeth Jones that he fathered her bastard child. He was brought to jail for want of bail. When Elizabeth Jones came to town, Robert Black agreed to marry her and did so Jun. 27, 1815, before a number of witnesses. Both of them had declared themselves free to marry at that time.

Apr. 20, 1820 - Depositions of Henry Hoffmyer [sic], Charles

Conley [sic], and George Matter were read to the court. The court then gave Sarah Black a divorce from her husband, Robert Black.

Lancaster Co., Pa., Appearance Docket Nov. Term 1819 #247 - Frances Trinque by her next friend, John Robinson, vs. Peter Trinque, libel in divorce. Original documents are now missing.

Lancaster Co., Pa., Appearance Docket Nov. Term 1819 #268 - Patrick Kelly vs. Bridget Kelly, libel in divorce.
Oct. 4, 1819 - Petition of Patrick Kelly who stated that he married Nov. of 1806 his present wife, Bridget. He lived with her for three years in Ireland then about nine years ago he moved to the U.S. intending to send for his wife later. He returned to Ireland five years later and found that about eighteen months prior to his return she had been guilty of adultery. Since then he has been informed that she has emigrated to York Co., Pa.
Oct. 4, 1819 - Court issued a subpoena for Bridget Kelly to appear in court to answer the libel of her husband, Patrick Kelly, for a divorce.
Lancaster Co., Pa., Appearance Docket Jan. Term 1820 #140 1/2 - Patrick Kelly vs. Bridget Kelly, libel in divorce.
Mar. 4, 1820 - Court appointed Jacob Beelor, Esq., to take depositions in this case.
Mar. 4, 1820 - Deposition of William Magawen, lately from the Parish of Clendavadog in the co. of Donegal, Ireland. He is well acquainted with Bridget Kelly. About six or seven years ago, he was present in the Roman Catholic Church in the Parish of Clendavadog when Bridget Kelly acknowledged she had a child "begotten in the bed of adultery" and rendered the church satisfaction. William Magawen then signed his petition "by mark."
Mar. 22, 1820 - Deposition of Hannah McEntire, lately from the Parish of Clandavady [sic], Co. of Donegal, Ireland, who was well acquainted with Bridget Kelly and was godmother of Bridget's only child now living that she had by Patrick Kelly. Bridget Kelly later had another child after her husband went to America by James Kelly of the same parish. She accompanied Bridget Kelly when she took the child to James Kelly and James Kelly did not deny that he was the father of the child. She was present at the Roman Catholic Church when both Bridget Kelly and James Kelly gave satisfication to the Roman Catholic Church as parents of a "child begotten in a bed of adultery." Hannah McEntire signed her deposition "by mark."
Mar. 25, 1820 - Deposition of Patrick Kelly that he imigrated from Ireland to America in 1810 with full consent of his wife, Bridget. Five years later he returned to Ireland and found that his wife had given herself up to adulterous practices.

Lancaster Co., Pa., Appearance Docket Jan. Term 1821 #5 - Bridget Kelly by her next friend, Barhard Friel, vs. Patrick Kelly, libel in divorce.

Aug. 24, 1820 - Petition of Bridget Kelly by her next friend, Barnard Friel, that she married Patrick Kelly, formerly of Ireland but now of Elizabethtown, Lancaster Co., Pa., about 1809. He left her without any support for herself and young child about 1816. In this year he threw her out of his house in Elizabethtown, leaving her in distressed circumstances. Testified before Jacob Peelor, justice of the peace of Lancaster Co., Pa. Bridget Kelly signed her petition "by mark."

Nov. 21, 1820 - Court issued a subpoena for Patrick Kelly to appear in court to answer the libel of his wife, Bridget Kelly, for a divorce. Sheriff reported he served the subpoena by copy and it took him eighteen miles to do so.

(Note - this may be the same Patrick Kelly involved in three other legal actions in Lancaster Co., Pa., in 1821. Aug. Term 1821 #19 was Patrick Kelly vs. William McGovern. Aug. Term 1821 #20 was Patrick Kelly vs. Sarah Smith. Aug. Term 1821 #21 was Patrick Kelly vs. Jacob Imhel.)

Lancaster Co., Pa., Appearance Docket Apr. Term 1821 #1 - Catharine Ruch by her next friend and brother, David Stoner, vs. Philip Ruch, libel in divorce.

Jan. 4, 1821 - Petition of Catharine Ruch (formerly Stoner) by her next friend and brother, David Stoner, of Manheim Twp., Lancaster Co., Pa. She married in Mar. of 1806 Philip Ruch. Four years and upwards ago he deserted her without cause leaving no provision for her or the seven children she bore to Philip Ruch. She wants Philip Ruch to appear in court on the third Monday of Apr. 1821 at 3 P.M. to answer her libel for a divorce. Testified before John Light, justice of the peace. Catharine Ruch signed her petition "by mark."

Jan. 15, 1821 - Court issued a subpoena to Philip Ruth [sic] to appear in court to answer the libel of his wife, Catharine Ruth [sic], for a divorce.

Lancaster Co., Pa., Appearance Docket Aug. Term 1821 #26 - Catharine Ruch by her next friend and brother, David Stoner, vs. Philip Ruch, libel in divorce.

Aug. 24, 1821 - Court appointed Daniel Moore, Esq., to take depositions in this case.

Sept. 5, 1821 - Deposition of John Shriner who said he was well acquainted with Catharine and Philip Ruch. Philip Ruch left his wife over four years ago without any cause and made no provision for his wife or his seven children.

Sept. 5, 1821 - Deposition of Henry Shriner which was identical with that of John Shriner.

Sept. 24, 1821 - Court was given proof of production of the *Lan-*

caster Journal for four weeks prior to Aug. Term 1821 requiring Philip Ruch to appear which he failed to do. Depositions of John Shriner and Henry Shriner were read to the court and the court granted Catharine Ruch a divorce from her husband, Philip Ruch.

Lancaster Co., Pa., Appearance Docket Apr. Term 1821 #9 - Ann Maria Dietrich by her next friend, Abraham Gochenauer, vs. Michael Dietrich, libel for divorce.

Jan. 18, 1821 - Petition of Anna [sic] Maria Dietrich (formerly Keyl) before Patton Boyd, recorder, by her next friend, Abraham Gochenauer. She married in Jun. of 1814 Michael Deitrich of Conestogoe Twp. son of Henry Deitrich of Conestogoe Twp., Lancaster Co., Pa. Her husband abused her and they separated about a year ago. Shortly before their separation "Michael labored under a foul disease, called the venerial and continued for a long time under the hands of three physcians [sic] at differant [sic] times." He also sold off most of his property leaving her a small part and then moved to his father's house. She requested the court to subpoena her husband to appear in court to answer her libel for divorce on the third Monday of Apr. 1821 at 3 P.M. Notation on the front of this petition states that the defendant lives with his father in Stumptown.

Jan. 19, 1821 - Petition of Anna [sic] Maria Dietrich was read and the court issued a subpoena for Michael Dietrich to appear in court to answer the libel of his wife, Ann Maria Dietrich, for a divorce. The sheriff reported he served this subpoena by copy and it took him four miles.

Lancaster Co., Pa., Appearance Docket Aug. Term 1821 #123 - Ann Maria Dietrich by her next friend, Abraham Gochenauer, vs. Michael Dietrich, libel in divorce.

Aug. 24, 1821 - Court appointed Daniel Moore, Esq., to take depositions in this case.

Sept. 1, 1821 - Deposition of Dr. Clarkson Freeman that Michael Dietrich called on him two or three times since his marriage for "the bad disorder and is hardly ever clear of it and got medicine from this deponant to cure the same."

Sept. 1, 1821 - Deposition of John Storrick, M.D., who stated that about two years ago Michael Dietrich called on him to cure "the pox" and didn't want his wife to know of it. He was addicted to excessive drinking. He refused to pay his bill claiming the doctor failed to cure him. He also said "the general report in the neighborhood was that Dietrich had given his wife the pox."

Sept. 24, 1821 - Proof given of notice for four successive weeks in the Lancaster Journal for Michael Dietrich to appear in court Aug. Term 1821 but he failed to do so. Court granted Ann Maria Dietrich a divorce from her husband Michael Dietrich.

Lancaster Co., Pa., Appearance Docket Apr. Term 1821 #66 - Mary Long by her next friend, William Miller, vs. Alexander Long, libel in divorce.

March 7, 1821 - Petition of Mary Long by her next friend, William Miller. She married on Aug. 9, 1810, Alexander Long. About Sept. 1, 1816, he abandoned her and made no provision for her maintenance thereafter.

Mar. 7, 1821 - Court issued a subpoena for Alexander Long to appear in court Apr. Term 1821 to answer the libel of his wife, Mary Long, for a divorce. E. Wright, atty. for libellant, and F.A. Muhlenberg, Esq., Prothy., signed this subpoena.

Lancaster Co., Pa., Appearance Docket Apr. Term 1821 #15 - Mary Long by her next friend, William Miller, vs. Alexander Long, libel in divorce.

Dec. 24, 1821 - Court appointed James Johnson, Esq., to take depositions. Original documents are now missing from this file.

Lancaster Co., Pa., Appearance Docket Aug. Term 1821 #33 - Catharine Fuhrman by her next friend, Esther Smith, vs. Conrad Fuhrman, libel in divorce.

May 9, 1821 - Petition of Catharine Fuhrman by her next friend, Esther Smith. She married Conrad Fuhrman, late of Lancaster Co. in May of 1810. He deserted her in May of 1812 without any just or reasonable cause. Catharine Fuhrman signed her petition "by mark."

May 9, 1821 - Court issued a subpoena for Conrad Fuhrman to appear in court for the Aug. Term 1821 to answer the libel of his wife, Catharine Fuhrman, for a divorce.

Lancaster Co., Pa., Appearance Docket Jan. Term 1822 #42 - Catharine Fuhrman by her next friend, Esther Smith vs. Conrad Fuhrman, libel in divorce.

Jan. 28, 1822 - Court appointed Benjamin Bauman, Esq., to take depositions in this case.

Jan. 28, 1822 - Deposition of Joseph Uhrich that Catharine Fuhrman was married to Conrad Fuhrman about twelve years ago. About a month later he abandoned her without cause for about two years. He then returned for about three or four weeks, then left again and has never returned.

Jan. 28, 1822 - Deposition of Samuel Wolf that Catharine Fuhrman was married to her present husband Conrad Fuhrman about twelve years ago. He lived with her only a few weeks then abandoned her without any good or sufficient cause to his knowledge.

Jan. 29, 1823 - Depositions or witnesses were read to the court and the court granted Catharine Fuhrman a divorce from her husband, Conrad Fuhrman. Cost was $5.34.

Lancaster Co., Pa., Appearance Docket Aug. Term 1821 #121 - Catharine Wilhelm by her next friend, Charles H. Cordes, vs. Charles Wilhelm, libel in divorce.

Jun. 20, 1821 - Petition of Catharine Wilhelm by her next friend, Charles H. Cordes, stated that she married Charles Wilhelm of the borough of Lancaster, Pa., and had three children. He deserted her nearly four years ago in Aug. of 1817 and she has not seen him since. She believes that he no longer lives in Lancaster Co., Pa. Catharine Wilhelm signed her petition "by mark."

Jun. 22, 1821 - Court issued a subpoena to Charles Wilhelm to appear in court to answer the libel of his wife, Catharine Wilhelm, for a divorce.

Lancaster Co., Pa., Appearance Docket Nov. Term 1821 #161 - Catharine Wilhelm by her next friend, Charles H. Cordes, vs. Charles Wilhelm, libel in divorce.

Dec. 29, 1821 - Court appointed Daniel Moore, Esq., to take depositions in this case.

Feb. 18, 1822 - Depositions read to the court and the court granted Catharine Wilhelm a divorce from her husband, Charles Wilhelm. Original documents are now missing which must include the depositions above mentioned.

Lancaster Co., Pa., Appearance Docket Jan. Term 1822 #3 - Rebecca Zell by her next friend, Caleb Jones, vs. John Zell, Esq., libel in divorce.

Nov. 12, 1821 - Petition of Rebecca Zell by her next friend, Caleb Jones, that she married on Mar. 6, 1810, John Zell, Esq., of the village of Churchtown, Carnarvon Twp., Lancaster Co., Pa. From Apr. 1, 1812, until Jun. 23, 1818, he abused her and thereby forced her to leave him. In fact he "turned her out of doors and therby forced her to withdraw from his house and family."

Nov. 19, 1821 - Court issued a subpoena to John Zell, Esq., to appear in court to answer the libel of his wife, Rebecca Zell, for a divorce. Sheriff reported that he had served the subpoena by copy and it took him twenty miles to do it.

Lancaster Co., Pa., Appearance Docket Jan. Term 1822 #4 - Jacob Brocke vs. Christiana Brocke, libel in divorce.

Nov. 12, 1821 - Petition of Jacob Brockey [sic] of Cocalico Twp., Lancaster Co., Pa. He married about Sept. of 1814 Christiana Weiss. She deserted him in Mar. of 1815 without any just or reasonable cause.

Nov. 12, 1821 - Court issued a subpoena for Christiana Brocke to appear in court to answer the libel of her husband, Jacob Brocke, for a divorce and the sheriff reported he traveled nineteen miles to serve it by leaving a copy.

Jan. 19, 1823 - Jacob Brocke denies all the allegations of his wife. He says he was a good husband and she left him without any just cause over six years ago. He requests a trial by jury.

Oct. 1, 1823 - Court appointed Jacob Hibschman, Esq., to take depositions in this case.

Lancaster Co., Pa., Appearance Docket Jan. Term 1822 #5 - Patrick Kelly vs. Bridget Kelly, libel in divorce.

Nov. 15, 1821 - Petition of Patrick Kelly of the village of Elizabethtown, Lancaster Co., Pa. He married his present wife Bridget in Nov. of 1806 and lived with her about three years in Ireland. He then came to America with his wife's consent intending to send for his family later. Five years later he returned to Ireland. In the meantime his wife Bridget had committed adultery and a child was born to her about eighteen months prior to his return to Ireland. Since then his wife has moved to Lancaster Co., Pa. He first applied for a divorce in Oct. of 1819 but was unable to obtain it because he was not a U.S. citizen. He is now a U.S. citizen and has paid the costs of the former proceedings and now wants a divorce!

Lancaster Co., Pa., Appearance Docket Apr. Term 1822 #35 - Patrick Kelly vs. Bridget Kelly, libel in divorce. Original documents in this file now missing.

Lancaster Co., Pa., Appearance Docket Jan. Term 1822 #8 - Catharine Dessinger by her next friend, Jonas Brown, vs. Peter Dessinger, libel in divorce.

Nov. 20, 1821 - Petition of Catharine Dessinger by her next friend, Jonas Brown. She stated that she married Peter Dessinger on Nov. 11, 1819. Her husband deserted her a few days later. Catharine stated that she was a native of Pa., and "has resided therein during her whole life." Catharine Dessinger signed her petition "by mark."

Nov. 21, 1821 - Court issued Peter Dessinger a subpoena to appear in court to answer the libel of his wife, Catharine Dessinger, for a divorce. The sheriff reported that he served this subpoena by leaving a copy of it and it required twelve miles of travel to do so.

Jan. 29, 1822 - Depositions were read and the court granted Catharine Dessinger a divorce from her husband, Peter Dessinger, and directed her ex-husband to pay the costs ($9.71).

Lancaster Co., Pa., Appearance Docket Jan. Term 1822 #43 - Daniel Cain vs. Christiana Cain, libel in divorce.

Nov. 23, 1821 - Petition of Daniel Cain that he married on Aug. 29, 1819, his present wife Christina [sic]. In Sept. of 1820 she abandoned him without any just cause, and she has for "a considerable time past given herself up to adulterous practices." Daniel Cain signed his petition "by mark."

Dec. 10, 1821 - The court issued a subpoena to Christina [sic]

Cain to appear in court to answer the libel of her husband, Daniel Cain, for a divorce.

Aug. 29, 1822 - Answer of Christiana Cain to her husband's libel for a divorce. She admitted that she married Daniel Cain Aug. 29, 1819, but she denied deserting her husband in Sept. of 1820. She accused Daniel Cain of committing adultery with a certain Ellen Connal at divers times between Jun. 1, 1820, and Aug. 1, 1822. Christiana Cain signed her answer "by mark."

Lancaster Co., Pa., Appearance Docket Jan. Term 1822 #46 - Stephen Steley vs. Nancy Steley, libel in divorce.

Dec. 10, 1821 - Petition of Stephen Steley that he married about nine years ago Nancy Kindig. In Mar. or Apr. of 1821 his wife married John Peham and continues to live with him knowing she is still legally married to her first husband, himself.

Dec. 14, 1821 - Court issued a subpoena to Nancy Steley to appear in court to answer the libel of her husband, Stephen Steley, for a divorce.

Lancaster Co., Pa., Appearance Docket Apr. Term 1822 #5 - John Miller vs. Nancy Miller, libel in divorce.

Jul. 14, 1821 - Petition of John Miller of Constagoe Twp., Lancaster Co., Pa., that he has been married to his present wife, Nancy Miller, for many years. She is guilty of adultery and "yet continues to be guilty of adulterous acts to the great shame and scandel [sic] of her family and of your petitioner."

Jan. 24, 1822 - Petition filed and the court issued a subpoena for Nancy Miller to appear in court to answer the libel of her husband, John Miller, for a divorce. Sheriff reported it required eight miles to serve this subpoena by copy.

Lancaster Co., Pa., Appearance Docket Apr. Term 1822 #65 - Elizabeth Caley by her next friend, Samuel Eberlein, vs. George Caley, libel in divorce.

Feb. 21, 1822 - Petition of Elizabeth Caley by her next friend, Samuel Eberlein. She married George Caley in Apr. of 1808. In 1816 he deserted her without a reasonable cause and continues to do so. She requests a subpoena for George Caley to appear in court on the third Monday of Apr. 1822. She testified this petition before Robert Spear.

Mar. 4, 1822 - Samuel Dale testified that the court issued a subpoena Mar. 4, 1822, for George Caley to appear in court to answer the libel of his wife, Elizabeth Caley, for a divorce. Sheriff reported that it took him ten miles to serve this subpoena by copy.

Sept. 16, 1822 - Defendant denies the facts stated in plaintiff's libel and requests the county make enquaries [sic] regarding them.

Sept. 29, 1823 - Jury of twelve men finds for the libellant and

grants Elizabeth Caley a divorce from her husband, George Caley.
Costs were $10.30.

Lancaster Co., Pa., Appearance Docket Apr. Term 1822 #22 -
Catharine Chew by her next friend, Philip Stockslegger, vs. William
Henry Chew, libel in divorce.

Mar. 4, 1822 - Petition of Catharine Chew by her next friend,
Philip Stockslegger, before William Bausman. She testified that she
married William Henry Chew on Nov. 6, 1808. In Jan. of 1818 her
husband deserted her and never returned. She requested a subpoena for him to appear in court at the next Apr. term. Both Catharine
Chew and Philip Stockslegger signed the petition "by mark."

Mar. 5, 1822 - Court issued a subpoena for William Henry Chew
to appear in court to answer the libel of his wife Catharine Chew for
a divorce. Contd. to Aug. Term 1822 #56.

Nov. 30, 1822 - Court appointed Daniel Moore, Esq., to take
depositions. "Plaintiff's death suggested." No further information
found on these depositions or the final result of this case.

Lancaster Co., Pa., Appearance Docket Apr. Term 1822 #75 -
Elizabeth Koehm by her next friend, George Rock, vs. John Koehm,
libel in divorce.

Mar. 9, 1822 - Petition of Elizabeth Koehm by her next friend,
George Rock, before James Clyde, justice of the peace of Lancaster
Co., Pa. She married John Koehm on Jul. 2, 1806, and he deserted
her in Aug. of 1818. She requested a subpoena be issued for John
Koehm to appear in court Apr. Term 1822.

Mar. 11, 1822 - Court issued a subpoena for John Koehm to
appear in court to answer the libel of his wife, Elizabeth Koehm, for
a divorce.

Lancaster Co., Pa., Appearance Docket Aug. Term 1822 #57 -
Elizabeth Koehm by her next friend, George S. Rock, vs. John
Koehm, libel in divorce.

Jan. 25, 1823 - Court appointed James Clyde, Esq., to take depositions in this case. Signed by Christ. Bachman for F.A. Muhlenberger, prothy.

Feb. 21, 1823 - Deposition of George Wikes, aged fifty years and
upwards, of the borough of Columbia, Pa., taken in the office of
James Clyde in the borough of Columbia, Pa. He was well acquainted with John and Elizabeth Koehm for eighteen years. He understood they were married about fifteen or sixteen years ago and lived
together about twelve years, during which time they had five or six
children. Sometime in 1818 John Koehm absented himself from his
wife and he has not heard anything of him ever since. Elizabeth
Koehm has lived in Pa. over eighteen years. George Wikes signed his
name in German script.

Feb. 21, 1823 - Deposition of Henry Martin of the borough of

Columbia, Pa., aged thirty-eight years and upwards. He knew John and Elizabeth Koehm seventeen years and upwards. He understood they were married fifteen or sixteen years ago and lived together nine or ten years during which time they had four or more children. In 1818 John Koehm left his family and never returned. Elizabeth Koehm has lived in Pa. for upwards of seventeen years.

Feb. 21, 1823 - Deposition of Elizabeth McNeal of the borough of Columbia, Pa., testified that she knew John and Elizabeth Koehm for fifteen years and upwards. She had heard John Koehm say that he married Elizabeth about sixteen or seventeen years ago. They lived together as man and wife for eleven or twelve years and had six children. In the summer of 1818 John Koehm absented himself and she has heard nothing of him since. His wife Elizabeth Koehm has lived in Columbia, Pa., ever since she knew her. Elizabeth McNeal signed her petition "by mark."

Feb. 21, 1823 - Deposition of Jacob Mathiot of the borough of Columbia, Pa., that she knew John and Elizabeth Koehm for seventeen or eighteen years. He understood they were married fifteen or sixteen years ago. They lived together eleven or twelve years and had five or six children. In the summer of 1818 John Koehm absented himself and he has not seen him or heard of him since. Elizabeth Koehm has lived in Pa. for seventeen years and upwards.

Feb. 25, 1823 - Depositions of witnesses were read to the court and the court granted Elizabeth Koehm a divorce from her husband, John Koehm. Costs were $9.464 [sic].

Lancaster Co., Pa., Appearance Docket Apr. Term 1822 #89 - Elizabeth Clark by her next friend, Robert Barber, vs. John Clark, libel in divorce.

Mar. 16, 1822 - Petition of Elizabeth Clark by her next friend, Robert Barber. She married John Clark on Nov. 12, 1786. He deserted her without any just cause in 1796. She requested the court to issue a subpoena for John Clark to appear in Court of Common Pleas of Lancaster Co., Pa., on the third Monday of Apr. Term 1822 to answer her libel.

Mar. 16, 1822 - Samuel Dale, judge of the Court of Common Pleas of Lancaster Co., Pa., issued a subpoena to John Clark to appear in court to answer the libel of his wife, Elizabeth Clark, for a divorce. Signed by E. Wright, atty. for libellant, and F.A. Muhlenberg, Esq., the prothy. of Lancaster Co., Pa.

Lancaster Co., Pa., Appearance Docket Aug. Term 1822 #88 - Elizabeth Clark by her next friend, Robert Barber, vs. John Clark, libel in divorce.

Nov. 30, 1822 - The court appointed Daniel Moore, Esq., to take depositions in this case. Signed by H.G. Long for F.A. Muhlenburg, prothy.

Dec. 20, 1822 - At the office of Daniel Moore, Esq., in Lancaster,

Pa., deposition of John Reitzel of the city of Lancaster, Pa., was made. He was acquainted with both John and Elizabeth Clark. Over twelve years ago John Clark abandoned her without any cause he knew of. He never returned to his wife.

Dec. 20, 1822 - At the office of Daniel Moore, Esq., in Lancaster, Pa., the deposition of Frederick Sweitzel was made. He knew John Clark and over twelve years ago he abandoned his wife without any just or reasonable cause and never returned. Frederick Sweitzel signed his deposition in German script. The fifty cents cost of the deposition was paid by E. Wright.

Dec. 23, 1822 - Depositions of witnesses were read to the court and the court granted Elizabeth Clark a divorce from her husband, John Clark. Cost was $9.774 [*sic*].

Lancaster Co., Pa., Appearance Docket Aug. Term 1822 #5 - Hetty Doak by her next friend, Henry Haines, vs. Robert Doak, libel in divorce.

Apr. 6, 1822 - Petition of Hetty Doak by her next friend, Henry Haines. She married about twenty-two years ago Robert Doke [*sic*]. Her husband abused her and she left him in Mar. of 1817 and then maintained herself and two of her children. Sworn before Samuel Dale.

Apr. 16, 1822 - Court issued a subpoena for Robert Doak to appear in court to answer the libel of his wife, Hetty Doak, for a divorce.

Lancaster Co., Pa., Appearance Docket Aug. Term 1822 #22 - Juliana Leiblen by her next friend, John Keller, vs. Mathias Leiblen. Subpoena for divorce from bed and board and for alimony. Original document now missing.

Lancaster Co., Pa., Appearance Docket Aug. Term 1822 #104 - John Patterson vs. Catharine Patterson, libel in divorce.

Jun. 15, 1822 - Catharina [*sic*] Patterson acknowledged that her husband, John Patterson, was entitled to a divorce and gave her consent. She signed "by mark." Witnesses were Jacob Miller and Jacob Leibly.

Jun. 17, 1822 - Petition of John Patterson who married his present wife Catharine on Oct. 22, 1812. She has given herself up to adulterous practices and had a bastard child by Valentine Hoffman who was duly convicted in Lancaster Co., Pa. Catharine Patterson later married on Oct. 11, 1818, Peter Adams. Sworn before Samuel Dale.

Jun. 22, 1822 - Court issued a subpoena to Catharine Patterson to appear in court to answer the libel of her husband John Patterson for a divorce.

Aug. 31, 1822 - Deposition read to the court and the court granted John Patterson a divorce from his wife, Catharine Patterson. Costs were $8.75.

Lancaster Co., Pa., Appearance Docket Nov. Term 1822 #57 - Magdalena Smith by her next friend, William Smith, vs. William Smith, Jr., libel in divorce.

Oct. 5, 1822 - Petition of Magdalena Smith, wife of William Smith [sic], late Magdalena Hoeffert, a daughter of John Hoeffert, by her next friend, William Smith. She married William Smith [sic] on Jul. 18, 1822. He abandoned her and had "nearly taken her life." He has been declared an habitual drunkard. He "has by his threats, and cruel and barbarous treatment endangered her life." This petition was sworn before Samuel Carpenter, alderman.

Oct. 17, 1822 - Court issued a subpoena to William Smith, Jr., to appear in court to answer the libel of his wife, Magdalena Smith, for a divorce. The sheriff reported he served this subpoena by first reading it and then leaving a copy with the defendant It required ten miles of travel on his part to do this.

Lancaster Co., Pa., Appearance Docket Jan. Term 1823 #6 - Esther Boyles by her next friend, George Brenneman, vs. John Boyles, libel in divorce.

Nov. 21, 1822 - Petition of Esther Boyles by her next friend, George Brenneman. She married on Dec. 17, 1815, John Boyles. On Nov. 1, 1819, she left him because of his abuse to her. Esther Boyles swore this before D. Moore and signed her petition "by mark."

Nov. 21, 1822 - Court issued a subpoena to John Boyles to appear in court to answer the libel of his wife, Esther Boyles, for a divorce.

Lancaster Co., Pa., Appearance Docket Apr. Term 1823 #20 - Esther Boyles by her next friend, George Brenneman, vs. John Boyles. Subpoena had been served by giving a copy to the defendant and it took the sheriff sixteen miles to do this.

May 5, 1823 - Court appointed George Hollinger, Esq., to take depositions in this case. Original documents in this file are now missing.

Lancaster Co., Pa., Appearance Docket Apr. Term 1823 #19 - Magdalena Weaver by her next friend, Henry Gettmacher, vs. John Weaver, libel in divorce.

Jan. 28, 1823 - Petition of Magdalena Weaver by her next friend, Henry Gettmacher. She married on Apr. 16, 1802, John Weaver. He deserted her in Oct. of 1819. She has been a resident of Pa. for more than eighteen years and she signed her petition "by mark."

Jan. 31, 1823 - Court issued a subpoena for John Weaver to appear in court to answer the libel of his wife, Magdalena Weaver, for a divorce.

Lancaster Co., Pa., Appearance Docket Aug. Term 1823 #122 - Magdalena Weaver by her next friend Henry Gettmacher vs. John Weaver, libel in divorce.

Dec. 27, 1823 - On motion of Mr. Wright, court appointed James Clyde, Esq., to take depositions. Signed H.G. Long for F.A. Muhlenberg, prothy.

Jan. 16, 1824 - Deposition of Jacob Geltmacher of West Hempfield Twp., Lancaster Co., Pa., who has known John and Magdalena Weaver twenty years and upwards. They were married over twenty years ago and lived together as man and wife until the sixteenth of Oct. in 1819 when John deserted his wife and continues to do so. Jacob Geltmacher signed his deposition in German script.

Jan. 16, 1824 - Deposition of Eve Sherks of the borough of Columbia, Pa., who had known John and Magdalena Weaver over five years. About the middle of Oct. 1819 John Weaver left his wife without any cause she knows of and has continued to absent himself.

Jan. 16, 1824 - James Clyde certified his depositions and indicated that he was paid 37 cents for his services.

Jan. 19, 1824 - Depositions of witnesses were read to the court and the court granted Magdalena Weaver a divorce from her husband, John Weaver.

Lancaster Co., Pa., Appearance Docket Aug. Term 1823 #9 - Catharine Bohmer vs. Andreas Bohmer, libel in divorce.

Mar. 24, 1823 - Petition of Catharina [sic] Bohmer before George Matter by her next friend and father, Peter Schwenk. She had married Mar. 13, 1815, Anrew Bohmer. Her husband deserted her about Oct. 1, 1815, without any reasonable cause. Catharina [sic] Bohmer signed her petition "by mark."

Apr. 26, 1823 - Court issued a subpoena to Andreas Bohmer to appear in court to answer the libel of his wife, Catharine Bohmer, for a divorce.

Lancaster Co., Pa., Appearance Docket Aug. Term 1823 #24 - Ann McDonald by her next friend, Thomas Elliott, vs. David McDonald, libel in divorce.

Apr. 26, 1823 - Petition of Anne McDonald by her next friend, Thomas Elliott. She married David McDonald about twenty years ago. His abuse has caused her to withdraw from him. Anne McDoanald testified this before Samuel Dale.

May 8, 1823 - Court issued a subpoena to David McDonald to appear in court to answer the libel of his wife, Ann McDonald, for a divorce.

Aug. 27, 1823 - Court appointed Daniel Moore, Esq., to take depositions in this case. On same day, Daniel Moore, Esq., gave notice to David McDonald that depositions of witnesses would be taken at his office in the city of Lancaster tomorrow Aug. 28, 1823, between 8 A.M. and 6 P.M. where he could attend to cross-examine the witnesses. This document was signed by J.B. Porter, atty. for libellant.

Aug. 28, 1823 - Ann McDonald testified that she served this notice on her husband, David McDonald, Aug. 27, 1823, by giving him a copy. She also said that she had a witness, Jno. Garretson, who was present between three and four years ago when David McDonald became very violent and pulled her out of bed where she had been confined for five days and she had an infant in bed with her. This witness is now sick at Abraham Herr's.

Aug. 28, 1823 - Deposition before D. Moore of Catharine Foster. She has lived in part of the house of Ann McDonald, city of Lancaster about three years. As "it will be three years and a half by next April." During this time Ann lived sometimes in this house and sometimes in other houses owned by her and her husband. Her husband was "sometimes in liquor." They frequently were quarreling. Last night David McDonald pulled his wife "Ann off the bench - caught her her by the throat and kicked her and said he would give her a blow yet that would keep her from going from home." He then watched her so close she "had to get a female to go home with her through the lot of this deponent and round about the sheets. That when the said David is in liquor he is very ill-natured and cross towards his wife and children and he is often in liquor, especially at night." Catharine Foster signed her deposition "by mark."

Aug. 28, 1823 - Deposition before D. Moore of Elizabeth Haines who had known Ann McDonald several years and lived the last three years in part of her house. Sometimes she would live with her husband and sometimes with her. "The said David McDonald was frequently in liquor especially in the evening and when in liqour [sic] would fight and quarrel with his said wife Ann McDonald, in consequence of which cruel treatment to her, she the said Ann would have to withdraw from his said house. That when the said Ann would be from home, on business, as she goes out to work, and is very industrious to make every cent she hopefully can, the said David would provide nothing for the children - and they would be in almost a starving condition. That during the last night, he the said David abused and maltreated the said Ann as is mentioned in the deposition of Catharine Foster." Elizabeth Haines signed her deposition "by mark."

Aug. 28, 1823 - Deposition of Catharine Boot before D. Moore who had known Ann McDonald for several years and for nearly three years has lived in part of her home. She said Ann McDonald's husband abused her and caused her to live sometimes with her. "He was frequently in liquor especially in the evening and when so he is very quarrelsome and would scold and abuse his said wife Ann McDonald and the children." He endangered her life and caused her to leave him. Ann McDonald "is very industrious hard working woman and endeavors to do well by her children but the said David neglects them and this deponent knows of the said Ann coming home frequently from working and on her complaining that he had neglected the children and that they were almost starving, he the said David would abuse her and she could not stay with him but would have to come over and stay in the house where deponent lives. That during last evening, about eight o'clock, he came over into the yard where Deponent lives, caught the said Ann by the throat, pulled her off the bench, and kicked her several times, until she made her excape [sic] from him. He then followed her up and she had to hid [sic] from him. He threatened that if he got hold of her he would break some of her bones, and prevent her from going from home to attend law suits." Catharine Boot signed her deposition "by mark."

Aug. 28, 1823 - Deposition before D. Moore of Barbara Roff who has known Ann McDonald several years and for over two years has lived in part of Ann McDonald's house. Ann McDonald had a special room furnished in this house where she could live whenever she was compelled to leave her husband. "David McDonald is very often in liquor and abuses his said wife Ann very much when he is so. She the said Ann is a very industrious hardworking woman and goes from home to endeavor to make all the money she profitably can. That on her coming home and finding that he the said David McDonald was doing no good and the children being nearly in a starving condition, when she would speak of it, he the said David McDonald would immediately abuse her in such a way, and offer such indignities to her person as to render her condition intolerable and life burthensome [sic], and thereby force her to withdraw from his house and family, and she would come over and reside in the house in which Deponent lives." Barbara Roff signed her deposition "by mark."

Aug. 28, 1823 - D. Moore testified that he took the depositions of four witnesses in this case between nine and eleven A.M. No person appeared to cross examine them.

Feb. 1, 1833 - On motion of Mr. Champney. Court appointed Samuel Dale, Esq., to take depositions in this case, signed by Christ. Bachman, prothy.

Feb. 27, 1833 - Samuel Dale gave notice to David McDonald of depositions to be taken Saturday Mar. 2, 1833, between ten and twelve A.M. at the office of Samuel Dale, city of Lancaster.

Mar. 2, 1833 - Ann McDonald testified that copy of commission and notice upon David McDonald which was served on him at his place of residence in Lancaster City with Mrs. Braderly.

Mar. 2, 1833 - Deposition of Jacob Dorwart that on Thursday, David McDonald mentioned to him he had received his notice to attend the depositions to be taken and he told him he would attend.

Mar. 2, 1833 - Deposition of James Stone that he was well acquainted with David McDonald in 1822 and the early part of 1823. At that time David McDonald was "in the habit of frequently becoming intoxicated. And when intoxicated abused and illtreated her and offered such indignities to her person as to render her condition intolerable and life burthensome, and thereby forced her to withdraw from his house and family. And she was compelled by his treatment of her and abuse of her person, to seperate [sic] herself and withdraw from him."

Mar. 2, 1833 - Depositions of Jacob Dorwart. He frequently heard Ann McDonald offer, that if her husband would stop drinking and abusing her "she would cheerfully maintain him and his family by her own exertions without any aid from him." He refused to do this and continued his drinking and abuse. Sixty-two and a half cents was paid by B. Chapney for depositions.

Lancaster Co., Pa., Appearance Docket Aug. Term 1823 #25 - Susanna Hudson by her next friend, Philip Beckerd, vs. John Hudson, libel in divorce.

Apr. 28, 1823 - Petition of Susanna Hudson of Caernarvon Twp., Lancaster Co., Pa., by her next friend, Philip Bechard [sic]. She married John Hudson in 1808. For a year and upwards he has deserted her and she believes he has been guilty of adultery. While living with him, he abused her and "repeatedly threatened her life." Susanna Hudson testified before D. Moore and signed her petition "by mark."

May 8, 1823 - Court issued a subpoena to John Hudson to appear in court to answer the libel of his wife, Susanna Hudson, for a divorce.

Aug. 25, 1823 - Court appointed Edward Davis, Esq., to take depositions in this case, on motion of Mr. Jenkins. Signed by H.G. Long for Mr. F.A. Muhlenberg, Esq. John Hudson was notified that examination of witnesses would take place before John Zell, Esq., in Churchtown on Monday, Oct. 6, 1823, at one P.M. They waited until 3 P.M. but John Hudson failed to appear.

Oct. 6, 1823 - Deposition of Jacob Mart who was well acquainted with John Hudson. Since the separation of John Hudson and his wife "he saw the said Hudson walking familiarly across the meadow with a woman who then kept house for him, with their arms round each other's waist, that he has seen the said Hudson drunk several times."

Oct. 6, 1823 - Deposition of William Hoar who was well acquainted with John Hudson. He and his wife parted in the summer of 1822. "He the deponant [sic] went to the said Hudson early one morning last fall, knocked at the door twice went in and found Hudson in bed and his housekeeper setting near the bed."

Oct. 6, 1823 - Deposition of John Becherd [sic] that John Hudson and his wife separated sometime in Mar. of 1822 and John did not provide for his wife after that. John told him that he suspected his wife of having "had criminal connection with other men." He also said he would have killed her with an axe had he not been prevented. At the request of Susanna Hudson's father he twice went to try to persuade John Hudson to take his wife back. John Hudson refused and said her father might keep her.

Oct. 6, 1823 - Deposition of Christian Eshelman that he lived near John Hudson in 1822 after his separation from his wife. "He has frequently passed deponant's [sic] house with a woman who then kept house for him on his arm, that deponent went home with him several times from Churchtown when he endeavorded [sic] to vex his wife by black guarding and telling her that he had such girls he liked better than her." Signed in German script.

Oct. 6, 1823 - Deposition of Michael Sergison who testified that while John Hudson lived with his wife he told him that he had a venereal disease and asked him to apply to the Dr. for some medicine. He got John Hudson some pills and mercury and gave them to him. Later John Hudson told him he was doctoring with Dr. Hudson.

Oct. 6, 1823 - Deposition of Dr. John McCamant who testified that in the fall of 1819 John Hudson told him he had the venereal disease and contracted it in Lancaster, Pa. He had first doctored with Dr. Gibson but the medicine didn't help. So, he gave John Hudson medicine. John Hudson said he thought his wife also had the disease and if so he would send her to him. They both came at different times until they were cured. "Hudson told the deponent he would never live with his wife again."

Dec. 27, 1823 - Depositions of witnesses were read to the court and the court granted Susanna Hudson a divorce from her husband, John Hudson.

Lancaster Co., Pa., Appearance Docket Aug. Term 1823 #51 - Sarah Burden by her next friend, Zebulon Payres, vs. Isaac Burden, libel in divorce.

Jun. 3, 1823 - Petition of Sarah Burden by her next friend, Zebulon Ayres [sic], that she married on Jun. 7, 1807, Isaac Burden who deserted her on May 13, 1823. For a considerable time past he had given himself up to adulterous practices and was guilty of adultery with a servant girl with whom he eloped. Testified before Samuel Dale.

Jun. 3, 1823 - Court issued a subpoena to Isaac Burden to appear in court to answer the libel of his wife, Sarah Burden, for a divorce.

Lancaster Co., Pa., Appearance Docket Nov. Term 1823 #37 - Sarah Burden by her next friend, Zebulon Ayers [sic], vs. Isaac Burden, libel in divorce.

Jan. 26, 1824 - Court appointed Samuel Dale, Esq., to take depositions in this case.

Jan. 31, 1824 - On motion of Mr. Champney, the court appointed Elias P. Seeley, Esq., of Bridgeton, N.J., to take depositions. Signed by Christian Bachman for F.A. Muhlenberg, prothy.

Mar. 1, 1824 - Deposition of Margaret Stogden at the office of Elias P. Seeley in Cumberland Co., N.J. She was late of Lancaster Co., Pa. - and now of Cumberland Co., N.J., aged twenty-three years. She had known Isaac Burden about twelve years. On Jul. 4, 1821, she moved from Cumberland Co., N.J., back to Lancaster Co., Pa., and lived part of the time with Isaac Burden's family. In Apr. of 1823 she moved back to Cumberland Co., N.J. On Aug. 10, 1823, in Cape May Co., N.J., she gave birth to a female bastard child. The child was conceived while she lived in the house of Isaac Burden and near the town of Strausburgh, Lancaster Co., Pa. "The child's father was Isaac Burden who was the only person to have had connection with her."

Lancaster Co., Pa., Appearance Docket Aug. Term 1823 #100 - Mary Nicholas by her next friend, Frederick Heberling, vs. Jacob Nicholas, libel in divorce.

Jul. 5, 1823 - Petition of Mary Nicholas by her next friend, Frederick Heberling. She was born as Mary Gantz in Lancaster Co., Pa., and has lived there all her life. She married on Feb. 24, 1805, Jacob Nicholas who "for a considerable time has given himself up to adulterous practices and been guilty of adultery and had criminal connection and intercourse with a certain Polly Crosby." Both Mary Nicholas and Frederick Heberling signed the petition in German script. Mary Nicholas testified before Samuel Dale.

Jul. 5, 1823 - Court issued a subpoena to Jacob Nicholas to appear in court to answer the libel of his wife, Mary Nicholas, for a divorce.

Lancaster Co., Pa., Appearance Docket Nov. Term 1823 #42 - Mary Nicholas by her next friend, Frederick Heberling, vs. Jacob Nicholas, libel in divorce.

Jan. 19, 1824 - On motion of Mr. Ellmaker the court appointed Jacob Graybill, Esq., to take depositions in this case. Signed by Christian Bachman for F.A. Muhlenberg, prothy.

Jan. 23, 1824 - Deposition or Henry Nicholas that Jacob Nicholas told him he would not stay with his wife as he had no love for her. He said he would go with another woman. Henry then told him "he would be glad to come back again and ask for a piece of bread and his reply was he would not. This deponent asked if he thought the child was his, his reply was yes it was. How do you know wether [sic] it was yours or not, where they were so many going. He said it was not true. She is not as bad as the peoples make her and this Deponent says he told Jacob Nicholas that you and your wife lived peacabl [*sic*] together and now all at once you go to live her and she kept herselve [*sic*] honorable and upright and he replyed [*sic*] that he would not stay any longer with his wife and further saith not."

Jan. 24, 1824 - Deposition of Henry B. Shaffner. "I spoke to Jacob Nicholas sometime after this dusturbance [*sic*] had taken place between him and his wife. I begd [*sic*] him to lay all aside what had taken place, and forsake that miss with which he had thy child. He told me he claimed they [*sic*] child to be his. I said perhaps he might be wrong (although) theire [*sic*] was no doubt she told you so. He signified that their [*sic*] was no doubt on his mind but he was they [*sic*] father. I said Jacob Nicholas I was told that your wife Mary is willing to take thy child home and raise it as if she was they [*sic*] mother, in case you would treat her as you use [*sic*] to treat her. Since you have lived together, except these seven last months. He had not been as affectionate to her as before. I begd [*sic*] him again to try and live together. He said he would not. He did not love her that is Mary Nicholas his wife. He would go with they [*sic*] other one, for he could not live with Mary his wife anymore in peace. Jealousy would allways [*sic*] exist between them. I told him no wonder I heard you asked leave of her, to go and see your miss every three weeks, or did you not. He said I can't leave her I love her. I replied to him give her up, your miss, and they [*sic*] peopel [*sic*] will forget it soon again. He said he would not live her [*sic*] any more. I replyed [*sic*] you will rue it. Your wife has allways [*sic*] been as far as your neighbors now [*sic*] a faithful woman, and a very good housekeeper. He said this was all very correct, but he could not live with her any more."

Jan. 24, 1824 - Deposition of Henry Haines, Jr., before Jacob Graybill, justice of the peace. Jacob Nicholos [*sic*] told him he would not live with his wife Mary. He said "my love is cold against her. I will go with another woman which hath a child to me for I love childern [*sic*]."

Jan. 27, 1824 - Deposition of Daniel Etter before Jacob Graybill, justice of the peace. He testified that Jacob Nicholas paid boarding for a Miss when she rented at his house in Mideltown [*sic*], Dauphin Co., Pa., - where he kept a public house. In Feb. or Mar. of 1823, Jacob Nicholas came to his house and called him to a room and told him he had something to say. He then told him "I have a Miss which is big with child to me and I want her som [*sic*] place to go, so no body [*sic*] find out for I want you to board her and at what you would charge me for her boarding. I told him one Dollar and seventy five cents. He told me that it was to [*sic*] much. She will eat with your family well. I will board her for one Dollar and fifty cents and he agreet [*sic*] for one Dollar and fifty cents per weeks and he paid me for they [*sic*] time she was there."

Jan. 28, 1824 - Depositions of witnesses were read to the court and the court granted Mary Nicholas a divorce from her husband, Jacob Nicholas.

Lancaster Co., Pa., Appearance Docket Nov. Term 1823 #82 - Elizabeth Bear by her next friend, Jacob Snyder, vs. Jacob Bear.

Oct. 22, 1823 - Petition of Elizabeth Bear by her next friend, Jacob Snyder. She married on April 6, 1809, Jacob Bear. He abused her and deserted her over twelve years ago without any reasonable or just cause. Elizabeth Bear signed her petition "by mark." Testified before John Reitzel.

Oct. 22, 1823 - Court issued a subpoena to Jacob Bear to appear in court to answer the libel of his wife, Elizabeth Bear, for a divorce.

Lancaster Co., Pa., Appearance Docket Jan. Term 1824 #46 - Elizabeth Bear by her next friend, Jacob Snyder vs. Jacob Bear, libel in divorce.

Apr. 21, 1824 - On motion of Mr. Porter, the court appointed John Reitzel, Esq., to take depositions. Signed by Christian Bachman for N.W. Sample, Jr., prothy.

Apr. 21, 1824 - Deposition of Nicholas Hartley who knew Elizabeth Bear lived at her father's for eight years and he never saw her husband then at the house of her father Jacob Erisman.

Apr. 21, 1824 - Deposition of George Martin who testified that Elizabeth Bear lived at her father's for eight years and he never saw her husband there during this time.

Apr. 21, 1824 - Deposition of Henry Christ who testified that Elizabeth Bear lived with her father more than six years and they are "his second door neighbor." He never saw her husband there during this time.

Apr. 21, 1824 - Deposition of Mrs. Margaret Fordney that about twelve years ago, Elizabeth Bear with her husband lived in the house of Mrs. Getz in the city of Lancaster and she lived in the same house. At that time Jacob left his wife and two children without providing for them at all. Sometime later he returned and sold all his goods. He never returned and Elizabeth went to live with her father where she lived until he died in Oct. of 1823 and she "continues to live in the City of Lancaster separate and apart from her said husband." Mrs. Margaret Fordney signed her deposition "by mark."

Apr. 21, 1824 - Deposition of Elizabeth Shindel that about fourteen or fifteen years ago Jacob and Elizabeth Bear after their marriage moved to the town of Strasburg, Pa. They lived there about nine months then moved to the Turnpike and lived there about a year and from there moved to Lancaster. Several years ago Jacob left his wife and even his father and friends didn't know where he was. Elizabeth Bear then lived with her father Jacob Erisman till he died in Oct. of 1823. Elizabeth Shindel signed her deposition in German script.

Apr. 23, 1824 - Court granted Elizabeth Bear a divorce from her husband, Jacob Bear.

Apr. 24, 1824 - Proof made that Jacob Bear was notified to appear in court by four weeks notice in the *Lancaster Intelligencer* but he failed to do so and court granted the divorce.

Lancaster Co., Pa., Appearance Docket Apr. Term 1824 #66 - Ann Auwerter by her next friend, Joel Lightner, Esq., vs. Leonard Auwerter, libel in divorce.

Apr. 19, 1824 - On motion of Mr. Ellmaker, the court appointed Daniel Moore, Esq., to take depositions in this case, signed by A.W. Sample, Jr., prothy.

Apr. 20, 1824 - Deposition of John Lightner, Esq., who was well acquainted with Leonard Auwerter and his wife Ann. They lived as man and wife in Londersburg, Pa., for fifteen years past. Sometime in Dec. of 1823 Leonard Auwerter told him he had kept a certain Ann York in the City of Lancaster, Pa., and had cohabited with her as man and wife from the time of Lechler's execution until then. He later moved to Philadelphia, Pa.

Apr. 20, 1824 - Deposition of Jonas Dorwart, Esq., who said that during last summer he frequently saw Leonard Auwerter sneaking about the house of Ann York and saw him go into her house about one or two P.M. When questioned about it he first said he did not know Ann York but then when it was mentioned that he was seen going into her house he "then said dam it I do not care who sees me going into her house. Said Ann York is a woman of loose and bad character."

Apr. 20, 1824 - Depostions of witnesses were read to the court and the court granted Ann Auwerter a divorce from her husband, Leonard Auwerter.

Lancaster Co., Pa., Appearance Docket Apr. Term 1824 #98 - Ann Gilmore by her next friend, John Morrison, Esq., vs. John Gilmore, libel in divorce.

Mar. 13, 1824 - Petition of Ann Gilmore by her next friend, John Morrison, Esq. She stated that on Jun. 2, 1819, she married John Gillmore [sic]. He deserted her without any just or reasonable cause in Sept. of 1819.

Mar. 13, 1824 - Court issued a subpoena to John Gilmore to appear in court to answer the libel of his wife Ann Gilmore for a divorce.

Lancaster Co., Pa., Appearance Docket Aug. Term 1824 #34 - Ann Gilmore by her next friend, John Morrison, Esq., vs. John Gilmore, libel in divorce.

Nov. 15, 1824 - Court appointed Daniel Moore, Esq., to take depositions in this case on motion of W. Jacobs.

Nov. 25, 1824 - Deposition of Jacob Rathfon who said Ann married John Gilmore in 1819 at his house. Sometimes in that said year John Gilmore ran away and deserted his wife. He has not been seen since and has not provided her any support.

Nov. 25, 1825 - Deposition of James Downey which stated the same basic facts as the previous deposition of Jacob Rathfon.

Lancaster Co., Pa., Appearance Docket Aug. Term 1824 #46 - Lydia Wallace by her next friend, David Heller, vs. David Wallace, libel in divorce.

Jun. 10, 1824 - Petition of Lydia Wallace by her next friend, David Heller, testified before Samuel Dale. She married David Wallace in Nov. of 1822. From Nov. 1, 1823, to May 27, 1824, he abused her and she was thereby forced to leave him on May 27, 1824.

Lancaster Co., Pa., Appearance Docket Aug. Term 1824 #83 - Jacob Usner vs. Catharine Usner, libel in divorce.

Jul. 3, 1824 - Petition of Jacob Usner who had been a resident of Pa., since birth. He married in 1814 Catherine Bieghart (Note - 1810 census shows a Jacob Bieghart living in Donegal Twp., Lancaster Co., Pa.). For a considerable time his wife had given herself up to adulterous practices and been guilty of adultery and had criminal connexcion [sic] with a certain Charles Brackerman.

Jul. 3, 1824 - Court issued a subpoena to Catharine Usner to appear in court to answer the libel of her husband Jacob Usner for a divorce, upon recommendation of Amos Ellmaker, atty. for libellant. Signed by Reah Frazer.

Lancaster Co., Pa., Appearance Docket Nov. Term 1824 #2 - Elizabeth When by her next friend, James Dunn, vs. John When, libel in divorce.

Aug. 17, 1824 - Petition of Elizabeth When by her next friend, James Dunn. She testified before Noah Lightner, alderman, that she married John When in 1809. He deserted her on Sept. 1, 1818. Statement was witnessed by William Johens and both James Dunn and Elizabeth When signed "by mark."

Aug. 17, 1824 - Court issued a subpoena to John When to appear in court to answer the libel of his wife, Elizabeth When, for a divorce. The sheriff reported "N.E.I. so answers Frederick Hambright, Shff."

Lancaster Co., Pa., Appearance Docket Nov. Term 1825 #36 - Elizabeth When by her next friend, James Dunn, vs. John When, libel for divorce.

Apr. 29, 1825 - Deposition of John Bassler before Nathaniel Lightner. He has known Elizabeth When since her childhood and her husband for the last ten years. They were married about sixteen years ago. Her husband left her about seven or eight years ago and has not rendered her any support thereafter. He doesn't know where John When now is. Filed Apr. 29, 1825.

Jan. 21, 1826 - On motion of Mr. Barr, the court appointed

Nathaniel Lightner to take depositions in this case.

Aug. 21, 1827 - Deposition was read and the court granted Elizabeth When a divorce from her husband, John When. Costs were
$3.50 for the prothy.; 37 cents for the sheriff; $3.00 for the atty.
which was already paid to Mr. Barr; $1.50 for the crier; and 37 cents
for the certificate; making a total cost of $8.74.

Lancaster Co., Pa., Appearance Docket Nov. Term 1824 #47 -
Sarah Backenstose by her next friend, John Morrison, vs. William
Backenstose, libel in divorce.

Oct. 4, 1824 - Petition of Sarah Backenstose before Samuel Dale
by her next friend, John Morrison. She married on Dec. 1, 1814,
William Backenstose of Lancaster Co., Pa. He deserted her without
any just cause in Sept. of 1821. Sarah Backenstone [sic] signed her
petition "by mark."

Oct. 5, 1824 - Court issued a subpoena for William Backenstose
to appear in court to answer the libel of his wife, Sarah Backenstone
[sic], for a divorce. E. Wright was the atty. for the libellant.

Lancaster Co., Pa., Appearance Docket Jan. Term 1825 #6 -
Sarah Backenstoce [sic] by her next friend, John Morrison, vs. William Backenstoce [sic], libel in divorce.

Jan. 22, 1825 - Court appointed Daniel Moore, Esq., and John
Mathiot, Esq., to take depositions in this case. Alias subpoena
issued and served by copy. Sheriff reported it took him eight miles
to do this. Original documents in this file are now missing.

Lancaster Co., Pa., Appearance Docket Nov. Term 1824 #50 -
Peter Smith vs. Susan Smith, libel in divorce.

Oct. 2, 1824 - Deposition of Christian Bassler of Manheim Twp.,
Lancaster Co., Pa., that Peter Smith is a resident of Pa. and has
always lived there.

Nov. 15, 1824 - On motion of Mr. Reigart the court appointed
Nathaniel Lightner, Esq., to take depositions in this case. Susan
Smith served notice of depositions when John Hambright left a copy
of this document with her.

Nov. 16, 1824 - Depositions to be taken at the office of Nathaniel
Lightner, Esq., Centre Square of Lancaster, Pa., between ten and
twelve o'clock Nov. 26, 1824.

Nov. 26, 1824 - Deposition of Henry M. Reigart of East Hempfield
Twp., Lancaster Co., Pa., that Susan Smith left her husband sometime between Oct. 1, 1822, and Oct. 8, 1822. "I am acquainted with
Peter Smith and know him to be a man of good charactor [sic]. Since
his wife left him, he worked for me all the winter following and since
that he worked for my Miller, and also in Donegal Township with one
Solomon Sellars." (Henry M. Reigart was paid $1.00 for testifying.)

Nov. 26, 1824 - Deposition of David Sechrist of Hempfield Twp. in
Lancaster Co., Pa., that "some time before the election of 1822 I went

to Peter Smith's wife's brother Jacob Grube. I took breakfast with him and after breakfast he went off, and I do not know where to, and I went away too and saw him walking, and about three-fourths of a mile I met him. We then went together towards Peter Smith's house, and Grube told me this morning there will be rough work, and I asked him what for, and he said Peter Smith's wife will leave him, and when we came to about twelve paces from Smith's house, she came towards us with a child in her arm. Then we went to the house and there John Grube's wife (Susan's sister-in-law) and others were packing up household furniture and goods. Then Grube asked where Peter Smith was and the people in the house said he was not at home but cutting wood at John Summys. Then Grube said this thing won't do and John Grube said it is all one if he knows it or not, we will load the goods and Jacob Grube said no he would go and bring Peter Smith. Then he went for him and brought him. Before Smith came they had loaded some goods and finished loading after Smith came they loaded and took away all the goods which Peter Smith's wife had brought when they got married, and his clothes I saw laying, that they did not take away. I heard Peter Smith say that it was a dirty trick of her friends and her to serve him this way without letting him know any thing of it. So far as I know him and from his general character in the neighborhood he is an honest and industrious man and the general opinion was that he was a good husband for her. The winter after Smith's wife left him he worked for Henry M. Reigarts. She was taken to her sisters, and where she lives now I can't tell. Peter Smith since then worked about the county and has for some time and now lives with Solomon Sellars at John Erb's Mill in Donegal Township."

Nov. 26, 1824 - Court granted Peter Smith a divorce from his wife, Susan Smith. Total cost was $9.07 of which $3.00 was for atty. fees.

Lancaster Co., Pa., Appearance Docket Jan. Term 1825 #14 1/2 - Rebecca Robinson by her next friend, George Youndt, vs. William Robinson, libel in divorce.

Dec. 3, 1824 - Petition of Rebecca Robinson before Henry D. Overholzer by her next friend, George Younde [sic]. She married on Feb. 19, 1822, William Robinson who gave her "cruel and barbarous treatment." He also endangered her life and in Oct. of 1822 he deserted her. Rebecca Robinson signed her petition "by mark."

Dec. 3, 1824 - Court issued a subpoena to William Robinson to appear in court to answer the libel of his wife, Rebecca Robinson, for a divorce. Sheriff reported he served this subpoena by copy and it took him twenty-three miles.

Apr. 20, 1825 - On motion of Mr. W. Jacobs the court appointed Henry D. Overhaltzer, Esq., to take depositions in this case. Signed by N.W. Sample, Jr., prothy., and Christ. Bachman.

Jun. 10, 1825 - Deposition of Daniel Schlenker who said that in the fall of 1822 he and Rebecca Robinson went to the house of William Robinson. "William seemed very anxious to speak with Rebecca but the women would not suffer them. They also struck with their fists upon the stove and said that she was not fit to keep house, and if it had not been for myself they would have struck her. We then left the house and the women still called after us and said if Mother was at home we would have not been suffered to come into the house."

Aug. 26, 1825 - Deposition of Susanna Meixel who said her daughter Rebecca married William Robinson sometime in Feb. of 1822. They lived as man and wife from April 1, 1822, until Sept. of 1822. Since then Rebecca has lived with her and her husband has not supported her at all. He husband deserted her and even while they lived together he only provided her with the barest of necessities. She had to give her of food or she would have starved to death while living with her husband. Her late husband Jacob Meixel took Rebecca to her husband's home after their separation but doors were locked and they were forbidden to enter. Susanna Meixel signed her deposition "by mark."

Aug. 26, 1825 - Deposition of Mary Lutz that Rebecca Meixil [sic] now Rebecca Robinson was married to William Robinson in Feb. of 1822. They lived together from Apr. of 1822 until the fall of 1822. Since then Rebecca has lived in her mother's family and been supported by her mother. She believes her husband totally neglected her. Soon after their separation she saw Rebecca and she appeared "half starved, lien [sic] and poor in body and very down hearted."

Aug. 31, 1825 - The court granted Rebecca Robinson a divorce from her husband, William Robinson.

Sept. 1, 1825 - Costs of divorce listed. Prot. $3.09; atty. fee $3.00; sheriff fee $2.84; and crier $1.50; making a total cost of $10.43.

Lancaster Co., Pa., Appearance Docket Jan. Term 1825 #16 - James G. Neale vs. Ann Catharine Neale, libel in divorce.

Dec. 7, 1824 - Petition of James G.W. Neale who married on Aug. 22, 1811, Ann Catharine Noeckly. She deserted him without any just cause on March 18, 1818. Sworn before Walter Franklin.

Jan. 19, 1825 - Court appointed Samuel Badger, Esq., to take depositions in this case at Philadelphia, Pa., and Col. Jacob Small to take depositions in this case at Baltimore, Md. Signed N.W. Sample, Jr., prothy., and Christ. Bachman.

Feb. 18, 1825 - Deposition of John N. Fisher who had known Ann Catharine Neale since her childhood and James G.W. Neale about twelve years. They have been married at least nine or ten years. For the last six or seven years Ann Catharine has lived in Northern Liberties Twp. in Philadelphia Co., Pa., apart from her husband.

They have not lived together since Ann Catharine returned from Baltimore which was six or seven years ago. James G.W. Neale lives in Lancaster, Pa., as he had a letter from him from there last Dec. Signed by S. Badger, alderman, and John N. Fisher.

Mar. 7, 1825 - Court replaced Col. Jacob Smith with William Crawford of the city of Baltimore to take depositions in this case.

Jun. 29, 1825 - Court granted James G.W. Neale a divorce from his wife Ann Catharine Neale. Costs were $2.50 for the prothy.; $1.50 for the crier; and 50 cents for a copy; making a total cost of $4.50.

Lancaster Co., Pa., Appearance Docket Apr. Term 1825 #75 - Lydia Hamilton by her next friend, William Steady, vs. John Hamilton, libel in divorce.

Feb. 28, 1825 - Petition of Lydia Hamilton before Nathaniel Lightner, mayor, by her next friend, William Steady. She stated that she married John Hamilton on Jan. 22, 1811, and he deserted her without any just cause in Jun. of 1811.

Mar. 21, 1825 - Court issued a subpoena to John Hamilton to appear in court to answer the libel of his wife Lydia Hamilton for a divorce.

Lancaster Co., Pa., Appearance Docket Aug. Term 1825 #8 - Lydia Hamilton by her next friend, William Steady, vs. John Hamilton, libel in divorce.

Apr. 29, 1825 - On motion of Mr. Jenkins the court appointed George Hoffman, Esq., to take the depositions in this case. Signed by N.W. Sample, Jr., prothy., and Christ. Bachman.

Jul. 16, 1825 - Deposition of Richard Ferree of Lampeter Twp., Lancaster Co., Pa., taken before George Hoffman, Esq., justice of the peace, in the borough of Strasburg, Pa. He knew both parties at the time of their marriage. John Hamilton left this neighborhood eight or nine years ago or more. Two or three years ago it was common report that John Hamilton was dead. Lydia Hamilton has always resided in this county except for four or five months and for the last seven or eight years has lived in his neighborhood as she still does.

Jul. 16, 1825 - Deposition of Isaac Evans of Lampeter Twp., Lancaster Co., Pa. He had known John and Lydia Hamilton since their marriage. John Hamilton left his wife and the neighborhood eight or nine years ago. "Perhaps more than two or three years ago it was currently reported that the said John Hamilton was dead." "That at another time there was a report that he had married again." Lydia Hamilton has continued to live in Lancaster Co., Pa., except for four or five months when she was in Chester Co., Pa. For seven or eight years Lydia Hamilton has lived in his neighborhood and she still does.

Dec. 21, 1825 - Court granted Lydia Hamilton a divorce from her husband, John Hamilton, on depositions of witnesses and non-appearance of John Hamilton even though notice had been published for his appearance on Sept. 23, 1825, and for four successive weeks thereafter. Costs were $3.50 to the prothy.; 37 cents for the sheriff; $3.00 for the atty.; $1.52 for the crier; and 50 cents for the certificate and copy; making a total cost of $8.87.

Lancaster Co., Pa., Appearance Docket Aug. Term 1825 #5 - Elizabeth Roy by her next friend, James Fleming, vs. Hugh Roy, libel in divorce.

Apr. 16, 1825 - Petition of Elizabeth Roy before Jacob S. Zell, justice of the peace, by her next friend, James Fleming. She married Hugh Roy in 1797. He deserted her without any just cause in 1805. Elizabeth Roy signed her name as "Margaret Roy."

Apr. 26, 1825 - Court issued a subpoena to Hugh Roy to appear in court to answer the libel of his wife, Elizabeth Roy, for a divorce.

Lancaster Co., Pa., Appearance Docket Nov. Term 1825 #37 - Elizabeth Roy by her next friend, James Flemming [sic], vs. Hugh Roy, libel in divorce. Sheriff reported he had served the subpoena on Hugh Roy and it took fifteen miles to do that.

Dec. 18, 1826 - On motion of Mr. Evans the court appointed Nathaniel Lightner, Esq., to take depositions in this case. Signed by N.W. Sample, Jr., prothy., and Christ. Bachman.

Dec. 18, 1826 - Deposition of James Fleming. He didn't know Hugh Roy but he knew Margaret Roy well. He lived with her in the same house for twelve years and he is certain Hugh Roy never visited her. "He verily believes he has not been heard of for many years."

Undated - Court granted Elizabeth Roy a divorce from her husband Hugh Roy. Costs were $4.01 for the prothy. and a copy of record; $3.00 for the atty.; and $1.57 for the sheriff; making a total cost of $8.57.

Lancaster Co., Pa., Appearance Docket Aug. Term 1825 #62 - Sarah Carter vs. John Carter, libel in divorce.

Jun. 14, 1825 - Petition of Sarah Carter of Lancaster Co., Pa., before Robert Spear, justice of the peace of Lancaster Co., Pa. She had lived in Pa. since birth and married John Carter in 1812. They lived together one year. She had two children by her husband. By his barbarous treatment she was obliged to leave him.

Jul. 14, 1825 - Court issued a subpoena to John Carter to appear in court to answer the libel of his wife, Sarah Carter, for a divorce.

Lancaster Co., Pa., Appearance Docket Nov. Term 1825 #32 - Elizabeth Hershey by her father and next friend, Christian Eggert, vs. Christian Hershey, Jr., libel in divorce.

Sept. 16, 1825 - Petition of Elizabeth Hershey before Samuel Dale. She married on March 28, 1814, Christian Hershey, Jr., of Rapho Twp., Lancaster Co., Pa. She left him on Dec. 2, 1823, because of his cruel and barbarous treatment. Elizabeth Hershey signed her name in German script.

Sept. 17, 1825 - Court issued a subpoena to Christian Hershey, Jr., to appear in court to answer the libel of his wife, Elizabeth Hershey, for a divorce. Sheriff reported that he served this subpeona by copy and to do so required eleven miles.

Dec. 19, 1825 - On motion of Mr. Wright, the court appointed Christian Strenge, Esq., to take depositions in this case. Signed N.W. Sample, Jr., prothy., and Christ. Bachman.

Jan. 7, 1826 - Deposition of Jacob Kauffman. Sometime in 1823 he heard Elizabeth Hershey holler for help while in her kitchen. He went into the kitchen and found her husband had violent hold of her by the neck and was treating her in a "most violent and abusive manner." He separated them and took Christian into the barroom [sic].

Jan. 16, 1826 - Deposition of John Haston taken at the office of Christian Strenge, Esq., at Petersburg, Hempfield Twp., Lancaster Co., Pa. He said that in Oct. or Nov. of 1823 he was standing in the street opposite the house of Christian Hershey. He saw Elizabeth Hershey leave her house crying. Christian came out immediately after and ordered her to go in to her work and asked her why she was crying. He could not hear her answer. Christian "then caught hold of his said wife with violence and attempted to pull her into the house. This affirmant then ran across the street and caught hold of the said Christian Hershey and pushed him against the post. The mother of the said Christian Hershey then called to this affirmant and begged him not to injure the said Christian Hershey. At another time this affirmant saw the said Christian Hershey throw into the street her bread baskets with the dough in them which his said wife had prepared for baking. This affirmant further saith that he has often heard the said Christian Hershey make use of the most vulgar profane and indecent language towards his said wife thereby rendering her life while she lived with him wretched, miserable and burthensome."

Jan. 31, 1826 - Deposition of Sarah Shallah. Sometime in 1823 Elizabeth Hershey left her husband because of his ill-treatment. She has often heard Christian abuse and ill treat Elizabeth "by beating her and pulling her hair and using the most indecent and un-becoming language." Sarah Shallah signed her deposition "by mark."

Jan. 31, 1826 - Court granted Elizabeth Hershey a divorce from her husband, Christian Hershey, Jr. Costs were $3.43 for the prothy.; $3.00 for the atty.; $1.88 for the sheriff; and $1.50 for the Cryer [sic]; making a total cost of $9.81.

Lancaster Co., Pa., Appearance Docket Apr. Term 1826 #9 - Harriet Kane by her next friend, Abraham Musser, vs. John W. Kane, libel in divorce. Her atty. was Mr. Slaymaker and his attys.

were W. Hopkins and R. Frazer.

Jan. 17, 1826 - Petition of Harriet Kane before Nathaniel Lightner, mayor, by her next friend, Abraham Musser. She married John W. Kane on June 13, 1824. On Dec. 22, 1825, she left him because he "did offer such indignities to her person as to render her condition intolerable and life burthensome and cruelly and barbarousely [*sic*] ill treated and endangered her life, without any just or reasonable cause and thereby forced her to withdraw from his house and family."

Jan. 21, 1826 - Court issued a subpoena to John W. Kane to appear in court to answer the libel of his wife, Harriet Kane, for a divorce. Sheriff reported he served this subpoena by copy and it took him one mile to do so.

Apr. 12, 1826 - John W. Kane by his atty. W. Hopkins filed a plea to the court stating he has never offered "such indignities to her person as to render her condition intolerable and life burthensome."

Lancaster Co., Pa., Appearance Docket Apr. Term 1826 #34 - Elizabeth Stormbach by her next friend, Jacob Lindy, vs. Anthony Stormbach, libel in divorce.

Feb. 7, 1826 - Petition of Elizabeth Stormbach before Samuel Dale by her next friend, Jacob Lindy. She married on Jan. 30, 1814, Anthony Stormbach. On Jan. 11, 1817, he deserted her without any just cause "leaving her and an infant daughter without any provision for her maintenance."

Feb. 21, 1826 - Court issued a subpoena to Anthony Stormbach to appear in court to answer the libel of his wife, Elizabeth Stormbach, for a divorce. Sheriff reported that he served this subpoena and it took him sixteen miles.

Lancaster Co., Pa., Appearance Docket Aug. Term 1826 #36 - Elizabeth Stormbach by her next friend, Jacob Lindy, vs. Anthony Stormbach, libel in divorce.

Dec. 18, 1826 - On motion of Mr. Wright, the court appointed John Mathiot, Esq., to take depositions in this case.

Dec. 23, 1826 - Deposition of Andrew Menold who saw Anthony Stormbach married Elizabeth Lindy sometime in 1814. Anthony Stormbach left his wife and infant child on Jan. 11, 1817, without any just cause and made no provision for their support.

Dec. 23, 1836 - Deposition of Susanna Menold who was present at the marriage of Anthony Stormbach to Elizabeth Lindy in 1814. On Jan. 11, 1817, he left his wife without any cause and continued absent from her. He made no provision for his wife or for his small infant child.

Dec. (day left blank), 1826 - Court granted Elizabeth Stormbach a divorce from her husband, Anthony Stormbach. Costs were $3.84 for the prothy.; $3.00 for the atty. E. Wright; 37 cents for the sheriff; and $1.50 for the crier making a total cost of $8.71.

Lancaster Co., Pa., Appearance Docket Apr. Term 1826 #37 - Margaret Gantz by her next friend, John Roland, vs. Michael Gantz, libel in divorce.

Feb. 23, 1826 - Petition of Margaret Gantz before Samuel Dale by her next friend, John Roland. She married on Jan. 4, 1806, Michael Gantz. He maliciously deserted her on Jun. 4, 1823. Since that time he never supported her or their family. She has always lived in Lancaster Co., Pa. Both Johannes Roland and Margaret Gantz signed "by mark."

Feb. 23, 1826 - Court issued a subpoena to Michael Gantz to appear in court to answer the libel of his wife, Margaret Gantz, for a divorce. Sheriff reported he served this subpoena and it took him sixteen miles to do so.

Lancaster Co., Pa., Appearance Docket Aug. Term 1826 #9 - Margaret Gantz by her next friend, John Roland, vs. Michael Gantz, libel in divorce.

Nov. 22, 1826 - Court shows that the sheriff published notice for appearance in court of Michael Gantz in the *Lancaster Telegraph*, a Lancaster, Pa. newspaper, for four successive weeks but he failed to appear in court. On motion of Mr. Ellmaker, the court appointed David May, Esq., to take depositions in this case. Signed by N.W. Sample, Jr., prothy.

Nov. 30, 1826 - Deposition of John Stauffer, yeoman, of Mt. Joy Township, Lancaster Co., Pa., before David May, Esq., justice of the peace. Michael and Margaret Gantz were his near neighbors for a number of years. He never heard anything to indicate that they did not live together peacefully. About three years ago, Michael Gantz abandoned his family and never returned. He has not heard of him being in Lancaster Co., Pa., but heard he went away with another woman. Lately he heard he was living in the state of Oh. As far as he knew "he had know [sic] reasonable cause for so doing."

Nov. 30, 1826 - Deposition of John Garman, carpenter, of Raphoe [sic] Twp., Lancaster Co., Pa. He was a near neighbor of Michael and Margaret Gantz for a number of years. He never heard anything indicating that they did not live peaceably together. About three years ago, Michael Gantz left his family and has never returned to Lancaster Co., Pa. since. He has heard he now lives in Oh. As far as he knew, he had no just or reasonable cause for leaving his wife and family.

Dec. 19, 1826 - Court granted Margaret Gantz a divorce from her husband, Michael Gantz. Costs were $3.50 for the prothy.; 37 cents for the sheriff; $3.00 for the atty.; and $1.50 for the crier; making a total cost of $8.37.

Lancaster Co., Pa., Appearance Docket Aug. Term 1826 #2 - Ann Paugle by her next friend, Christian Martin, vs. John Paugle, libel in divorce.

Apr. 17, 1826 - Petition of Ann Paugle, the wife of John Paugle, late of Manor Twp., Lancaster Co., Pa., taylor [sic], by her next friend, Christian Martin. She married John Paugle about thirteen years ago. Over two years ago he deserted her without any reasonable cause. Her petition was sworn before Patton Ross, recorder of the city of Lancaster, Pa.

Apr. 17, 1826 - Court issued a subpoena to John Paugle to appear in court to answer the libel of his wife, Ann Paugle, for a divorce.

Lancaster Co., Pa., Appearance Docket Nov. Term 1826 #22 - Ann Paugle by her next friend, Christian Martin, vs. John Paugle, libel in divorce.

Dec. 2, 1826 - Court appointed Nathaniel Lightner, Esq., to take depositions in this case. Signed by N.W. Sample, Jr., prothy., and Christian Bachman.

Dec. 14, 1826 - Deposition of Christian Martin who was well acquainted with John and Ann Paugle. He deserted her over two years ago without a reasonable cause and has continued absent from her. He has no knowledge of where John Paugle now is.

Dec. 14, 1826 - Deposition of Christian Hertzler who was well acquainted with John and Ann Paugle. John Paugle deserted his wife over two years ago without any reasonable cause. He has not been in the neighborhood ever since and he doesn't know "where he is or what has become of him." Filed Jan. 15, 1827.

Jan. 15, 1827 - Court granted Ann Paugle a divorce from her husband, John Paugle. Costs were $3.84 for the prothy.; $1.50 for the crier; 37 cents for the sheriff; and 37 1/2 cents for a copy making a total cost of $6.08 1/2.

Lancaster Co., Pa., Appearance Docket Nov. Term 1826 #11 - Matthias Hauk vs. Maria Hauk, late Maria Urban, libel in divorce.

Sept. 6, 1826 - Petition of Mathias Hauck [sic] of Cocalico Twp., Lancaster Co., Pa., before Samuel Dale. He married on Jun. 6, 1824, his present wife Maria. He was not told then but later discovered she already had a living husband, one Jacob Urban. At the time of her marriage she was known as Maria Urban but he didn't know she had a living husband.

Sept. 6, 1826 - Court issued a subpoena to Maria Hauk to appear in court to answer the libel of her husband, Matthias Hauk, for a divorce.

Lancaster Co., Pa., Appearance Docket Jan. Term 1827 #5 - Matthias Hauck [sic] vs. Maria Hauck [sic], late Maria Urban, libel in divorce.

Apr. 25, 1827 - On motion of Mr. Champneys, the court appointed John Mathiot, Esq., to take depositions in this case.

Undated - William White, sheriff, reports that since the return of the alias subpoena of Jan. Term 1827 he caused notice to be published in *Political Setinel* and *Lancaster Literary Gazette* two Lancaster, Pa. newspapers for four successive weeks prior to the first day of Apr. Term 1827 requiring the appearance of Maria Hauck [sic] in court.

Jun. 19, 1827 - Deposition of George Keller. He came from Bassel in Germany with Jacob Urban and his wife, Ann Maria Urban, in Mar. of 1817. He remained in Philadelphia, Pa. while Urban and his wife went to York Co., Pa., in August of 1817 to serve three years with Daniel Grose, farmer, to pay their passage. My brother served with him. She had a child during the passage. They arrived in York Co., Pa., in August of 1817. Maria Urban served her three years but her husband served only eighteen months then ran away from his master. He saw Maria Urban about five or six years ago at Strasburg and asked her where her husband was. "She said hush don't say anything about it. I want to get a better man. I want to pass myself off as a single lady that never was married. I said that she should take care of herself for if she ever married again she might get into trouble and at this she laughed and said nothing." George Keller signed his name in German script.

Jun. 19, 1827 - Deposition of Conrad Bowmiller. He was present on Jun. 3, 1825, when Mathias Hauck [sic] was married to Maria Urban by Rev. W. Endress. The couple went to Oh. He returned in Feb. of 1826 without his wife. She had promised to come in the spring but didn't. Hauck [sic] told him he never would have married her had he known she had been married before and he told him he had left her out in Oh. because she told him that she had been married before. Filed Jun. 19, 1827.

Jun. 19, 1827 - Court granted Matthias Hauck [sic] a divorce from his wife, Maria Hauck [sic]. Costs were $3.84 for the prothy.; $3.00 for the atty.; 37 cents for the sheriff; $1.50 for the crier; and 25 cents for the certificate; making a total cost of $8.96.

Lancaster Co., Pa., Appearance Docket Apr. Term 1827 #19 - Mary C. Barrett by her next friend, Sarah Gibbons, vs. Robert Barrett, libel in divorce.

Feb. 1, 1827 - Petition of Mary C. Barrett by her next friend, Sarah Gibbons, before Samuel Dale. She married on Aug. 29, 1822, Robert Barrett. "Within a few weeks of their marriage her husband commenced a course of cruel and barbarous treatment such as to endanger her life and repeatedly offered such indignities to her person as to render her condition intolerable, and life burthensome, and thereby forced her to withdraw from his house. The said Robert, during the first year of the marriage repeatedly struck, choked and kicked this libelalant [sic], that these instances of barbarous treatment were preceded by abusive language and that his angry passions gradually increased until they produced kicking and choking. That this conduct in most instances, was exhibited toward this libellant without any provocation on her part, without even replying to his abusive language. That this libellant resided in the State of Va., with her husband the said Robert, from the time of her marriage, until the fall of the year 1825. That during this period of time, the said Robert beat, chocked [sic] and kicked this libellant at least one hundred times. That the said Robert often attempted to injure the character of this libellant both before her face and behind her back, by saying those things that were false and scandalous and by applying to her all the epithets which are usually applyed [sic] to the most abandoned females, and that the said conduct appeared to proceed from a dispostion [sic] to agravate [sic] the feelings of this libellant. That the said Robert, after his most barbarous and abusive treatment of this libellant, would generally appear to be conscious of the injustice and cruelty of his conduct and acknowledge that this libellant had not deserved it. That what he had said was with a view of provoking her and that he knew it was false and did not believe it, and would promise at such time to conduct himself better. That this disposition of the said Robert generally lasted for about half a day, when he would again commence abusive language against this libellant. That during the time they resided in Virginia the said Robert was absent from home a considerable portion of his time in some instances a whole week at once. That notwithstanding this occasional absence the conduct of the said Robert became so intollerable [sic] of this libellant, that she was forced to separate from him and accordingly sent for her brother residing in the State of Pennsylvania to take her to her friends and relatives residing in the City of Lancaster, to which place she removed in the fall of 1825. That in about two weeks after the arrival of this libellant in the City of Lancaster the said Robert followed her and by his fair promises persuaded her again to live with him, which she continued to do, from the time of Christmas in 1825 to the beginning of the year 1827, when she was again forced by his continued barbarous and unfeeling conduct to withdraw from his house and society. That during the time of their residence in Lancaster, the conduct of the said Robert was as oppresive [sic] and intolerable to this libellant as it had been with the exception of it being accompanied with less violence, from which he was probably restrained by the circumstance of this libellant being surrounded by her friends. That however during the year 1826, the said Robert began quarreling with this libellant one night after they were in bed. That this libellant got up and went to another bed. That the said Robert soon followed, pulled her out of bed and violently thrust her out of doors. That this libellant went into the house of the intention of taking away her close [sic]. That the said Robert then said he was only in fun, acknowledged that it was his bad temper that prompted him to treat her in the manner he had done, entreated her not to leave him and even got down on his knees pleading with her to give him another trial. That in another instance during their residence in Lancaster the said Robert threw a case knife at this libellant, which glanced and struck a plate and broke it to pieces. That the said Robert then attempted to strike her, but this libellant avoided the blow and the said Robert struck the wall of the room."

Mar. 2, 1827 - Court issued a subpoena to Robert Barrett to appear in court to answer the libel of his wife, Mary C. Barrett, for a divorce.

Lancaster Co., Pa., Appearance Docket Aug. Term 1827 #4 - Mary C. Barrett by her next friend, Sarah Gibbons, vs. Robert Barrett, libel in divorce.

Mar. 12, 1828 - On motion of Mr. Fuller, the court appointed Mathew W. Kelly, Esq., alderman of Lancaster, Pa., to take depositions in this case. Signed by N.W. Sample, Jr., prothy., and Christian Bachman.

Mar. 15, 1828 - Deposition of James Donnelly who said Robert Barrett had told him and others that in Va. he had thrown his wife out of his house after night. "There was a number of steps from his ground up to the doorsill and he acknowledged that he had thrown her over the whole of them and that she got hold of a locust tree when falling to save herself. He acknowledged to me that he had offered her for sale to a man in Virginia. Her mother went out to Virginia for her and brought her to Lancaster County in consequence, as I have been told by the mother of his bad treatment of her. Mrs. Barrett did return to Lancaster with her mother. Barrett followed her to Lancaster sometime afterwards."

Mar. 15, 1828 - Deposition of James McNaughton that "I have frequently heard Robert Barrett say that he would be dammed if he would live with his wife. I heard him, one Sunday morning, in Lancaster, cursing his wife, and abusing her, and using ill language towards her. I have known Mrs. Barrett for a number of years and always knew her to sustain a good character. I know that Mrs. Barrett's mother went to Virginia and brought her to Lancaster in consequence of having heard he had ill-treated her. Barrett followed soon after and through the persuasions of her friends, she was persuaded to live with him again. Barrett told me at the time he left this place that he would be married before three weeks, after he would be in Virginia. That he would be dammed if he would not be married to a lady in Virginia. He said if Mary, his wife, thought that he had come here to hinder her from obtaining a divorce, she was mistaken. That he would be dammed if he would hinder her in any way from obtaining a divorce."

Mar. 15, 1828 - Deposition of Henry Donnelly that "I have heard Robert Barrett say that he had thrown his wife out of the house, in Virginia, and had treated her badly. That there were steps up to the door. That he had thrown her over them, and that she had caught hold of a locust tree, when falling, to save herself. It runs in my mind that he said if she had not caught hold of the tree, the fall would have hurted [*sic*] her, or killed her, or something to that effect."

Mar. 20, 1828 - Deposition of Isabella Killian that "the first that I heard of Barrett's ill-treatment of Mary was about two years ago or better. She wrote a letter on the subject to her sister Nancy, who is now dead. They kept the letter concealed from me for about two weeks. I then found it out, I was much troubled. I went off to Virginia. The neighbors there told me that Barrett treated her very badly. She said she could not live with him - that he turned her out of doors in the winter - that he kicked her and beat her - both in and out of the house. The neighbors told me the same thing. I brought her to Lancaster. I have often heard Barrett cast up to her that she was too intimate with Dr. Edwards, in Virginia. He was jealous of her and Dr. Edwards. I know he attended the family as a physcian, but he lived seven miles off, was a very decent, honest man and never was more than half a dozen times in his life in the house. Barrett followed her to Lancaster, about three weeks after she came. He wanted her to live with him but she refused. The neighbors and myself persuaded her and she did take up with him. They lived in the house that I had rented. I never saw a man treat a woman as badly as he did. He was afraid to beat her before me, but he would at night, pince [*sic*] and choak [*sic*] her. He would sometimes turn her out of the house at night. He once turned me out of the house at night. He often told me he would be damned if he would kill her. At the time he came back to Lancaster he took an oath that he would never again strike her. He always quarrelled with her about the victuals. It seemed that he begruged [*sic*] her the victuals. He was very passionate - a man of most violent passions. Once I came in from Mr. Landis and Mary cooked some eggs and made some tea for me. He came home and found three eggs missing. He called her a damed [*sic*] bitch and said that he would kill her and put her from eating eggs. I never saw or heard her say a cross word to him." Isabella Killian signed her deposition "by mark."

Mar. 20, 1828 - Deposition of Margaret Sommers that "when Mrs. Barrett came from Virginia, she and her mother lived in the house with me in Lancaster. I was one who persuaded her to live with him. At that time he swore that he would never again beat her, or strike her. I never saw anything improper about her conduct. She attended well to him. She kept him nice and clean. He told me that he would soon have another wife - that he had one bespoke in Virginia. Mary told me that he had thrown her down the steps in Virginia - that he kicked her into the house - made her go to bed - took a razor down and she expected he was going to cut her throat and that she lay quiet and would as soon have died as lived. I have often heard him say he would give up all right and title to her - that he would never again live with her. He was a man of violent temper and I have often heard him scolding and abusing her." Margaret Sommers signed her deposition "by mark."

Apr. 28, 1828 - Court granted Mary C. Barrett a divorce from her husband, Robert Barrett. Costs were $3.84 for the prothy.; $3.00 for the atty.; $1.26 for the sheriff and $1.50 for the crier; making a total cost of $9.60.

Lancaster Co., Pa., Appearance Docket Apr. Term 1827 #20 - Susan McCullough by her next friend, Abner Thomas, vs. Thomas McCullough, libel in divorce.

Jan. 15, 1827 - Petition of Susan McCullough by her next friend, Abner Thomas, before William Child. Susan married on Apr. 16, 1807, Thomas McCullough. He deserted her on Mar. 30, 1823, and thereafter has "given himself up to adulterous practices and been guilty of adultery." Susan McCullough signed her name Susan McCullouch. Filed Mar. 2, 1827.

Mar. 2, 1827 - Court issued a subpeona to Thomas McCullough to appear in court to answer the libel of his wife, Susan McCullough, for a divorce.

Lancaster Co., Pa., Appearance Docket Nov. Term 1827 #35 - Susanna McCullough by her next friend, Abner Thomas, vs. Thomas McCullough, libel in divorce.

Feb. 2, 1825 - Court appointed Thomas Dickey, Esq., to take depositions in this case.

Apr. 29, 1828 - Deposition of Henry Eagle of the village of Maytown, Lancaster Co., Pa., who had known Thomas McCullough upward of twenty years. Thomas McCullough married Susanna Fowler and they kept house both in Elizabethtown and Maytown. He left her more than two years ago. She brought a suit against him in Indiana Co., Pa., for her maintenance and he was summoned as a witness in her behalf and attended the court in Indiana Co., Pa., Tuesday, Mar. 28, 1826. Her husband denied the marriage but a jury found him guilty - From the testimony given to that court it appeared that he cohabited with another woman. He testified that Susanna McCullough has always had a good character.

Apr. 29, 1828 - Deposition of Samuel Bailie, Esq., of the borough of Marietta, Pa., who has known Thomas McCullough about twenty years. He knew Thomas and Elizabeth McCullough lived together both in Elizabethtown and Columbia. He left her some three years ago and continued absent. His wife he "considered her to always be a respectable woman. After her husband left her, my family were the instigation of her coming to Marietta to teach a school, for her support."

May 1, 1828 - Proclamation made and the court granted Susanna McCullough a divorce from her husband, Thomas McCullough. Costs were $3.84 for the prothy.; $3.00 for the atty.; $1.06 for the sheriff; and $1.50 for the crier making a total cost of $9.40.

Lancaster Co., Pa., Appearance Docket Apr. Term 1827 #30 - William McKnight vs. Eve McKnight, libel in divorce.

Mar. 16, 1827 - Petition of William McKnight before Walter Franklin. He married on Sept. 6, 1823, Eve Haines in the Gaol [*sic*] of Lancaster Co., Pa., while he was a prisoner there because Eve Haines had accused him of fornication and bastardy. After their marriage, Eve went to her own house and neglected to live with him. Since their marriage Eve has been guilty "of adultery in various instances and openly cohabits with other men."

Mar. 16, 1827 - Court issued a subpoena to Eve McKnight to appear in court for Apr. Term 1827 to answer the libel of her husband, William McKnight, for a divorce. E. Wright was the atty. for the libellant. Signed by N.W. Sample, Esq., prothy., and Walter Franklin. Continued to Aug. Term 1827 #14 (document missing).

Lancaster Co., Pa., Appearance Docket Aug. Term 1827 #3 - Leah Templeton by her next friend, Jacob Varnes, vs. James Templeton, libel in divorce.

Apr. 23, 1827 - Petition of Leah Templeton by her next friend, Jacob Varnes, before D. Moore. She married in Mar. of 1824 James Templeton and he maliciously deserted her in Nov. of 1824 without any just or reasonable cause. Leah Templeton signed her petition "by mark."

Apr. 24, 1827 - Court issued a subpoena to James Templeton to appear in court to answer the libel of his wife, Leah Templeton, for a divorce.

Lancaster Co., Pa., Appearance Docket Aug. Term 1827 #38 - Susanna Erhart by her next friends, David Kolp and George Fisher, vs. Henry Erhart, libel in divorce.

May 31, 1827 - Petition of Susanna Erhart by her next friends, David Kolp and George Fisher, before Samuel Dale. She married in 1799 Henry Erhart who now lives in Mt. Joy Twp., Lancaster Co., Pa. For many years he abused her and rendered her condition intolerable and life burthensome and thereby caused her to leave him.

May 31, 1827 - Court issued a subpoena to Henry Erhart to appear in court to answer the libel of his wife, Susanna Erhart, for a divorce. Sheriff reported he served this subpoena by copy and it required him to travel twelve miles to do so.

Aug. 22, 1827 - Court appointed Robert Richardson, Esq., to take depositions in this case. Signed by N.W. Sample, Jr., prothy., and Christ. Bachman.

Sept. 8, 1827 - "The deposition of David Colp of the Township of Mount Joy in the County of Lancaster produced and affirmed before me Robt. Richardson, Esq. one of the Justices of the Peace in and for the County of Lancaster agreable [*sic*] to a Rule from the Court of

Common Pleas directed to me the subscriber to take depositions of witnesses on a certain case of Divorce where Susan Earhart [sic] is the Plaintiff and Henry Earhart [sic] is Defendant. The said affirmant doeth depose and say that he is acquainted with Henry Earhart [sic] for ten years or there about and that for some years past he the said Henry Earhart [sic] has been in the habit of drunkness [sic] and has not made provision for his family and said Henry Earhart [sic] has called his wife a hoer [sic] and would whip her if she would not leave of going to publick [sic] worship [sic] with the Methodis [sic] Society and said affirmant informed said Henry Earhart [sic] that such threats would not doo [sic] he must do beter [sic] or theire [sic] must be something done. He informed said Earhart [sic] if he thought his wife was inconstant the said H. Earhart [sic] staited [sic] to said affirmant that he thought his wife was an honast [sic] womman [sic] but he would not give hir [sic] that satisfaction as he wanted to trubel [sic] hir [sic] and further Mrs. Susana [sic] Earhart [sic] is a prudant [sic] woman and a good housekeeper as far as I am acquented [sic] with hir [sic] and further saith not. Affirmed and subscribed this 8th day of September A.D. 1827." Signed by David Kolp and Robt. Richardson.

Sept. 8, 1827 - "The deposition of Elizabeth Hock of the Township of Donegal in the County of Lancaster produced and affirmed before me the subscriber Robt. Richardson, Esq. one of the Justices of the Peace in and for the said County agreable [sic] to a Rule issued from the Court of Common Pleas of Lancaster County directing me the said Justice to take depositions on behalf of aplicant [sic] on case of Devorse [sic] where Susana Earhart [sic] is Plaintiff vs. Henry Earhart [sic] is Defendant. The affirmant doeth depose and say that she has been acquanted [sic] with Henry Earhart [sic] about three years and during said time he has not provided for his family and he is a habitual drunkard and his conduct was unbecomingly cross in his family and Mrs. Earhart [sic] had to leave hir [sic] house for fear of hir [sic] husband. He came to the house where I lived hunting Mrs. Earhart [sic] three times in a [sic] angry manner in one night and went with a light to the garret and often called hir [sic] a laer [sic] and said he would whip hir [sic] if she would not come from the camp meting [sic] on a sabath day in May last when he suspected hir [sic] to be at meting [sic] and had a whip in his hand. She was not there. His behevaur [sic] towards his neighbors is unbecoming for abuse, disturbing the peace. He at one time did tear his cap in a angrey [sic] manner of [sic] hir [sic] head and at said time he gave hir [sic] a stroak [sic] on the head and further Mrs. Susana [sic] Earhart [sic] as far as I ever was acquented [sic] with hir [sic] is a deasent [sic] and prudant womman [sic] and a kind mother, a good house keeper [sic] and further saith not. Affirmed and subscribed this 8th day of September A.D. 1827 before me." Signed Robt. Richardson and Elizabeth Hock by "hir [sic] mark."

Sept. 8, 1827 - "The affirmation of Margreat [*sic*] Bradey [*sic*] of the Township of Donegal in the County of Lancaster prodused [*sic*] and affirmed before me Robt. Richardson, Esq. one of the Justices of the Peace in and for said county agreable [*sic*] to a rule issued from the Court of Common Pleas of Lancaster County to me the subscriber directing me to take depositions of witnesses in a certain action of Devorse [*sic*] now pending before said coart [*sic*] where Susana [*sic*] Earhart [*sic*] is Plaintiff and Henry Earhart [*sic*] is Defendant. She the said affirmant doeth depose and say that on the sabeth [*sic*] day some time [*sic*] in the month of May last she the said affirmant did see Henry Earhart [*sic*] folow [*sic*] Mrs. Earhart [*sic*] with a whip in his hand and did threaton [*sic*] Mrs. Earhart [*sic*] if she would go to the camp meting [*sic*] that he would whip hir [*sic*] and further that the Henry Earhart [*sic*] was a drunkard and further said affirmant doeth say that Mrs. Earhart [*sic*] is a prudant deasant [*sic*] womman [*sic*] as far as I know. Affirmed and subscribed this eight of September 1827 before me." Signed by Robt. Richardson and Margaret Brady.

Sept. 8, 1827 - "The deposition of Henry Rainder [*sic*] of the Township of Donegal in the County of Lancaster produced and affirmed before me the subscriber Robt. Richardson, Esq. one of the Justices of the Peace in and for the said County agreable [*sic*] to a rule issued frome [*sic*] the Coart [*sic*] of Common Pleas of Lancaster County to me directed to take depositions of witnesses in a certain action of devorse [*sic*] now pending before said coart [*sic*] where Susana [*sic*] Earhart [*sic*] is the complainent vs. Henry Earhart [*sic*]. He the said affirmant doeth depose and say that he is aquented [*sic*] with Henry Earhart [*sic*] about teen [*sic*] years and for some years past he Henry Earhart [*sic*] has been a habitual drunkard and further has not suported his family by his industrey [*sic*] and further did threaton [*sic*] his wife if she would go to meeting he would abuse hir [*sic*] and often did threaton [*sic*] his family and if Mrs. Earhart [*sic*] would put him to jail he would murder hir [*sic*] and the family that is if she Mrs. Earhart [*sic*] would swear the peace against him on such threats Mrs. Earhart [*sic*] left hir [*sic*] house and family and often cauled [*sic*] hir [*sic*] a lude [*sic*] womman [*sic*]. As far as I ame [*sic*] aquented [*sic*] with Mrs. Earhart [*sic*] she has been a prudant industrous [*sic*] womman (as) as I have lived in the family and further saith not. Affirmed and subscribed this 8th of September 1827 before me." Signed Robt. Richardson and Henry Bender.

Sept. 8, 1827 - "The deposition of Ann Brant of the Township of Londondary in the County of Dauphen [*sic*] prodused [*sic*] and affirmed before me Robt. Richardson, Esq. one of the Justices of the Peace in and for the County of Lancaster agreable [*sic*] to a Rule issued from the Coart [*sic*] of Common Pleas of Lancaster County to me directed to take depositions of witnesses in a certain case of Divorse [*sic*] now pending before said coart [*sic*] where Susana [*sic*]

Earhart [*sic*] is plaintiff and Henry Earhart [*sic*] is defendant. She the said affirmant doeth depose and say that she is aqunted [*sic*] with Henry Earhart about three years during said time he did not make provision for his family and was a habitual drunkard during said time and often times [*sic*] drove hir [*sic*] frome [*sic*] hir [*sic*] house for saiftey [*sic*] as she was affraid [*sic*] of him and often caled [*sic*] hir [*sic*] a lude [*sic*] womman [*sic*] and often did threton [*sic*] to abuse hir [*sic*] and often did threaton hir [*sic*] if she would go to hear the Methodests [*sic*]. He would kick hir [*sic*] and his family was often in terror when he was intoxicated as he was generely [*sic*]. So when he could have money or credit to get liquor and further Mrs. Earhart [*sic*] I ame [*sic*] acquented [*sic*] with during said term of three years and belive [*sic*] hir [*sic*] to be a prudant [*sic*] and vertious [*sic*] womman [*sic*] and a good house keeper [*sic*] and kind to hir [*sic*] family and further saith not. Affirmed and subscribed this eight day of September A.D. 1827 before me." Signed by Robt. Richardson and Ann Brant by "hir [*sic*] mark."

Sept. 8, 1827 - "The deposition of James McCarron of the Township of Mount Joy in the County of Lancaster prodused [*sic*] on his solemn oath before me Robt. Richardson, Esq. one of the Justices of the Peace in and for said County agreable [*sic*] to a Rule issued frome [*sic*] the Coart [*sic*] of Common Pleas of Lancaster County directing me the said Justice to take depositions of witnesses in a ceartain [*sic*] case of devorse [*sic*] where Susana [*sic*] Earhart [*sic*] is plaintiff vs. Henry Earhart [*sic*] defendant. The said deponent doeth depose and say that he has been aquented [*sic*] with Henry Earhart about two years and says that Henry Earhart [*sic*] was in the habit of abusing his wife and family and was a habitual drunkard and did not provide aney [*sic*] suport [*sic*] for his family and further Mrs. Earhart [*sic*] made hir [*sic*] escape to my house for saiftey [*sic*] and he Henry Earhart [*sic*] pursued hir [*sic*] to my house and put two pannels out of the door of my house to get in as the doar [*sic*] was locked to get in to his wife to abuse hir [*sic*]. At another time Mrs. Earhart [*sic*] was in my house and Henry Earhart [*sic*] split boards with his ax [*sic*] and swore he would split everey [*sic*] bord [*sic*] in my house if his wife would not come out of my house. As for Mrs. Earhart [*sic*] she is an industrous [*sic*] prudent womman [*sic*] as far as I know and further saith not. Sworn and subscribed this 8th day of September A.D. 1827 before me." Signed James McCarron by "his mark."

Sept. 8, 1827 - "The deposition of Cathrin [*sic*] McCarron in the Township of Mount Joy in the County of Lancaster prodused [*sic*] on hir [*sic*] solemn oath before me Robt. Richardson, Esq. one of the Justices of the Peace in and for said County agreable [*sic*] to a Rule isued [*sic*] from the Coart [*sic*] of Common Pleas of Lancaster (County) to me directed to take depositions of witness [*sic*] in a certain case of Devorse [*sic*] where Susana [*sic*] Earhart [*sic*] is plaintiff vs. Henry

Earhart [*sic*] is defendant. She the said deponent has been aquented [*sic*] with Henry Earhart [*sic*] for two years and believes that he did not make anney [*sic*] provision for his family's suport [*sic*] during said time and that he was a habitual drunkard and spent his arning [*sic*] and as far as his credit would be acpted [*sic*] in liquar [*sic*]. He was cross in his familey [*sic*] and Mrs. Eahart [*sic*] has came to my house for saiftey [*sic*] and he had the gun. She, Mrs. Earhart [*sic*] staited [*sic*] to said deponent that she was affraid [*sic*] that H. Earhart [*sic*] would shute [*sic*] hir [*sic*]. It was about 2 o'clock in the morning. Mrs. Earhart [*sic*] is a prudant [*sic*] industreaus [*sic*] and kind mother and a good house keeper [*sic*] and further saith not. Sworn and subscribed this 8th day of September A.D. 1827 before me." Signed by Robt. Richardson and Cathrin McCarron by "hir [*sic*] Mark."

Sept. 8, 1827 - "I certify the above depositions to be taken before me the subscriber sighned [*sic*] by said witnesses on theire [*sic*] affirmations or oaths taken the 8th day of September A.D. 1827 before me." Signed by Robt. Richardson. Costs were justices cost $2.10; Justice seven qualefications [*sic*] 21 cents; Justice account in full $2.31; and witnesses $2.70; making a total cost in suit of $5.01. Mileage for witnesses was E. Hock, 37 1/2 miles; James McCarron, 31 1/4 miles; Cathrin McCarron, 31 1/4 miles; David Colp, 37 1/2 miles; Ann Brant, 69 miles; Margrat [*sic*] Bradey, 31 1/4 miles and Henry Bainder, 31 1/4 miles.

Sept. 22, 1827 - Court granted Susanna Erhart a divorce from her husband Henry Erhart. Costs were $3.09 for the prothy.; $3.00 for the atty.; $1.50 for the crier; and $1.36 for the sheriff making a total cost of $9.55.

Lancaster Co., Pa., Appearance Docket Aug. Term 1827 #47 - Sarah Doyle by her next friend, David Mourer, vs. Patrick Doyle, libel in divorce.

Jun. 22, 1827 - Petition of Sarah Doyle by her next friend, Daniel Mourer, before Jacob Rohrer. She married on Nov. 28, 1818, Patrick Doyle. He abused her and she was thereby forced to leave him on Apr. 13, 1827.

Jul. 5, 1827 - Court issued a subpoena to Patrick Doyle to appear in court to answer the libel of his wife, Sarah Doyle, for a divorce. Signed by N.W. Sample, Jr., prothy., and Walter Franklin.

Aug. 28, 1827 - On motion of W. Barr, the court appointed Jacob Rohrer, Esq., to take depositions in this case.

Nov. 23, 1827 - Application of Sarah Doyle to be divorced was denied by the court.

Feb. 11, 1828 - Answer of Patrick Doyle to his wife's libel was that he was indeed married to Sarah but he treated her as a good husband should. However Sarah neglected to perform the duties which she was bound to by her marriage vow. He said she left not because of his mistreatment "but to gratify her own wayward and wanton disposition and because she was indisposed to perform any of the household duties of a wife." Filed Jun. 28, 1828.

Lancaster Co., Pa., Appearance Docket Jan. Term 1828 #26 - Sarah Doyle by her next friend, Daniel Mourer, vs. Patrick Doyle, libel in divorce.

Undated - Sheriff reported he had served a subpoena on Patrick Doyle by copy and it required twelve miles of travel on his part to do so.

Apr. 19, 1833 - On motion of Henry Long, Esq. Court appointed Robert Richardson, Esq., to take depositions in this case.

Apr. 24, 1833 - To Patrick Doyle from Robert Richardson, justice of the peace, depositions of witnesses to be taken in the office of Robt. Richardson in the village of Mt. Joy on Saturday, May 4, 1833, between one o'clock and five o'clock.

May 4, 1833 - Deposition of Daniel Maurer that Patrick C. Doyle left his wife Sarah upwards of six years past and has not provided any maintenance for her. Patrick C. Doyle now has a life in Richland and two children by him and also two basdert [sic] children in the town of Springville. All four children were born after he left his wife.

May 4, 1833 - Deposition of Margaret Brady of the town of Richland, Lancaster Co., Pa. Said Patrick C. Doyle left his wife upwards of six years ago. He left her with no support. He now lives with a womman [sic] which is said to be his wife and they have three children and also has three basdard [sic] children in the town of Springville all born after he left his wife.

May 4, 1833 - Deposition of Sarah Zell of the town of Richland, Lancaster Co., Pa., who has been acquainted with Sarah Doyle for four years. During the time her husband Patrick C. Doyle has lived separate from his wife and has not supported her. The present woman Patrick C. Doyle lives with told the deponant [sic] when she Mrs. Doyle was in childbirth "that hir [sic] and Patrick C. Doyle was married fore [sic] years and has three children in said time." "Said deponant has lived near neighborhood nearly too [sic] years with said Patrick C. Doyle and he and hir [sic] lives as man and wife and further saith not."

May 6, 1833 - Deposition of James Johnston of the town of Richland, Lancaster Co., Pa. Patrick C. Doyle has lived separate from his wife upwards of six years "and in said time has not to best of his knowledge given anney [sic] support for hir [sic]. He Patrick C. Doyle has a womman [sic] who he lives with as a wife. They have three children in the town of Richland."

Jun. 4, 1833 - On motion of Mr. Long, court granted a rule on defendant to show cause why divorce should not be granted. Exit rule dre [sic].

Jan. 29, 1835 - On motion of Mr. Long, court granted rule on respondent to answer libel of libellant on or before third Monday in Mar. of 1835. Contd. Term to Term until Nov. Term 1835.

Nov. 23, 1835 - Jury called - Samuel McKinney, Benjamin Miller, Martin Nisley, Peter Fahnestock, Daniel Kendig, Martin Miller, David Rinhehart, Jacob Bear, John Gochenauer, Joseph Grebill, Daniel Balmer, and Michael Wenger. Complainant withdrew the complaint and jury was discharged.

Lancaster Co., Pa., Appearance Docket Aug. Term 1827 #49 - Sarah Dietrick by her next friend, Edward Powell, Jr., vs. Lawrence Dietrick, libel in divorce.

Jul. 9, 1827 - Petition of Sarah Detrick [sic] before Samuel Dale by her next friend, Edward Powell, Jr. She married on Jan. 4, 1820, Lawrence Dietrich [sic]. He left her and their two infant children without any just or reasonable cause about April 1, 1823. He made no provision at all for her family. Sarah Detrich [sic] signed her petition "by mark."

Jul. 9, 1827 - Court issued a subpoena to Lawrence Dietrick to appear in court to answer the libel of his wife Sarah Dietrick for a divorce.

Lancaster Co., Pa., Appearance Docket Nov. Term 1827 #16 - Sarah Dietrich [sic] by her next friend, Edward Powell, vs. Lawrence Dietrich [sic], libel in divorce.

Undated - Sheriff reported he had tried to serve the subpoena on Lawrence Dietrich and it required one mile of travel on his part.

Dec. 28, 1827 - Court appointed John Mathiot, Esq., to take depositions in this case.

Apr. 26, 1828 - Deposition of John Powell, Jr., that Lawrence Dietrich married Sarah Powell about seven or eight years ago. He deserted her about four years ago without any just cause. He treated her in a barbarous and inhuman manner. "He made no provision for his family, and their personal property was sold for the satisfaction of his debts. That he was given to habits of intemperance and paid no regard to his family. That he the said Lawrence Dietrich has not been heard of for some years. That he the Deponent does not know where the said Dietrich [sic] now is."

Apr. 26, 1828 - Deposition of George Clickner who was acquainted with Lawrence Dietrich [sic] and his wife eight years last past. Some three years ago Lawrence left his family without any just or reasonable cause. "He has seen the said Lawrence very much in liquor a number of times."

May 2, 1828 - Court granted Sarah Dietrich [sic] a divorce from her husband, Lawrence Dietrich [sic].

Lancaster Co., Pa., Appearance Docket Nov. Term 1827 #12 - Elizabeth Kauffman by her next friend, Jacob Heiss, vs. John Kauffman, libel in divorce.

Aug. 7, 1827 - Petition of Elizabeth Kauffman of Leacock Twp., Lancaster Co., Pa., who married on Nov. 7, 1818, John Kauffman. They had three children. Her husband deserted his family about four years ago and left them with no support at all. She is informed he went to Oh.

Aug. 7, 1827 - Court issued a subpoena to John Kauffman to appear in court to answer the libel of his wife, Elizabeth Kauffman, for a divorce. Sheriff reported he served this subpoena and it required fourteen miles travel on his part to do so.

Lancaster Co., Pa., Appearance Docket Jan. Term 1828 #10 - Elizabeth Kauffman by her next friend, Jacob Heiss, vs. John Kauffman, libel in divorce.

Feb. 16, 1828 - On motion of W.L. Frazier, court appointed Samuel Dale, Esq., to take depositions in this case.

Apr. 12, 1828 - Deposition of George Mearing of Leacock Twp., Lancaster Co., Pa., well acquainted with John and Elizabeth Kauffman. They formerly lived about one mile from him. More than five years ago John left his wife and three small children. About two years later he came back into the neighborhood about three days and then again went away and never came back. He deserted his wife willfully and maliciously "without any reasonable cause given him by her."

Apr. 12, 1828 - Deposition of John Mearing of Leacock Twp., Lancaster Co., Pa., acquainted with Elizabeth Kauffman since her infancy. Her husband John Kauffman left her then about two years later he came back into the neighborhood about three days and then left again. He left his wife to support herself and her children and he deserted her without any reasonable cause given by his said wife.

Apr. 26, 1828 - Depositions were read to the court and the court granted Elizbeth Kauffman a divorce from her husband, John Kauffman. Costs were $3.84 for the prothy.; $3.00 for the atty.; and $1.50 for the crier making a total cost of $8.34 which was paid to prothy. N.W. Sample, May 1, 1828, by R. Frazer, Esq., plus $1.33 of the sheriff's costs paid to the prothy.

Lancaster Co., Pa., Appearance Docket Nov. Term 1827 #18 - Susanna Bitterman by her next friend, Jacob Binely, vs. Henry Bitterman, libel in divorce.

Aug. 4, 1827 - Petition of Susannah [sic] Bitterman by her next friend, Jacob Binely. She was married to Henry Bitterman on March 24, 1807. He mistreated her so badly that she was forced to leave him. Susannah [sic] Bitterman signed her petition "by mark."

Aug. 4, 1827 - Court issued a subpoena to Henry Bitterman to appear in court to answer the libel of his wife, Susanna Bitterman, for a divorce. Sheriff reported he served this subpoena and it required thirteen miles of travel to do this.

Lancaster Co., Pa., Appearance Docket Jan. Term 1828 #24 -

Susanna Bitterman by her next friend, Jacob Binely, vs. Henry Bitterman, libel in divorce.

Dec. 28, 1827 - On motion of John Markley, Esq., of the borough of Strasburg, Pa., was appointed to take depositions in this case by the court.

Undated - Sheriff reported he had served the subpoena on Henry Bitterman and it required fifteen miles travel to do this. Original documents in this file are now missing.

Lancaster Co., Pa., Appearance Docket Nov. Term 1827 #21 - Susanna Gilbert by her next friend, Valentine Hoffman, vs. Jacob Gilbert, libel in divorce.

Aug. 1, 1827 - Petition of Susanna Gilbert of the city of Lancaster that she married Jacob Gilbert on June 14, 1821, by James N. Barker, Esq., alderman in the city of Philadelphia, Pa. Previous to her marriage and afterwards she has always lived in the city of Lancaster, Pa. Jacob Gilbert never lived with her. He "very soon after the marriage offered such indignities to her person as to render her condition intolerable." He then deserted her without any just or reasonable cause.

Aug. 1, 1827 - Court issued a subpoena to Jacob Gilbert to appear in court to answer the libel of his wife, Susanna Gilbert, for a divorce. Sheriff reported that it required one mile of travel to serve this subpoena.

Lancaster Co., Pa., Appearance Docket Jan. Term 1828 #35 - Susanna Gilbert by her next friend, Valentine Hoffman, vs. Jacob Gilbert, libel in divorce.

Undated - Sheriff reported he had served the subpoena on Jacob Gilbert and it required fifteen miles travel on his part to do so.

Sept. 22, 1832 - On motion of Mr. Barton, court appointed Israel Carpenter to take depositions in this case.

Sept. 27, 1832 - Deposition of Gilbert D. Lowe of the city of Lancaster, Pa., who has known Susanna Gilbert to live in Lancaster, Pa., since her marriage seven or eight years ago. He knows her husband has never lived with her. Within a few days after their marriage they had an altercation in the streets of Philadelphia, Pa., which required a magistrate to settle. He attacked his wife to get "from her a sum of money." The attack was so violent as to attract a crowd of twenty to thirty people. "She offered to give him up the money in the magistrate's office provided he would swear that it was his which he declined doing." She testified Susanna Gilbert "has always been a remarkable steady and sober woman and has always been very kind in her family."

Sept. 27, 1832 - Deposition of Henry Lyne of the city of Lancaster, Pa. He was acquainted with Susanna Gilbert about five years. Her husband never lived with her. As far as I know he lives in the state of Md. He called Susanna "a very kind clever woman in her family and very sober and steady."

Sept. 28, 1832 - Depositions read to the court and sheriff had caused notice to be published in the *Lancaster Journal* a Lancaster, Pa. newspaper. Court granted Susanna Gilbert a divorce from her husband, Jacob Gilbert. Costs were $1.50 to prothy. S.; $2.34 to prothy. B.; $3.00 to the atty.; $1.57 for the sheriff; $1.50 for the crier, M. Zahn, Jr.; and 50 cents for a copy; making a total cost of $10.41 paid to prothy. on Oct. 3, 1832.

Lancaster Co., Pa., Appearance Docket Nov. Term 1827 #25 - Barbara Mull by her next friend, Isaac Mull, vs. Gerhart Mull, libel in divorce.

Nov. 20, 1827 - Court appointed Daniel Moore, Esq., to take depositions in this case. Original documents are now missing which include apparently the depositions gathered for this case.

Nov. 20, 1827 - Court granted Barbara Mull a divorce from her husband Gerhart Mull. Costs were $3.09 for the prothy.; $3.00 for the atty.; $1.50 for the crier; and 37 1/2 cents for the certificate; making a total cost of $7.96 1/2.

Lancaster Co., Pa., Appearance Docket Nov. Term 1827 #34 - Elizabeth Gochenour by her next friend, Isaac Graft, vs. John Gochenour, libel in divorce.

Aug. 15, 1824 - Petition of Elizabeth Gochenour by her next friend, Isaac Graft. About sixteen years ago she married John Gochenour. Upwards of four years ago, John Gochenour "wilfully and maliciously deserted and absented himself from her the said Elizabeth" without any just or reasonable cause. Elizabeth Gochenour signed her petition "by mark."

Aug. 15, 1824 - Court issued a subpoena for John Gochenour to appear in court to answer the libel of his wife, Elizabeth Gochenour, for a divorce. Sheriff reported he served this subpoena by copy and it required seven miles of travel to do so.

Dec. 1, 1827 - On motion of W. Heckert, court appointed John Mathiot, Esq., to take depositions in this case.

Dec. 12, 1827 - Deposition of John Eckman who had known John Gochenour and his wife, Elizabeth Gochenour, formerly Elizabeth Graft, for about eight years. They lived together as man and wife until "about four years ago, and then he left her and her habitation without any reasonable cause and has not resided with her since.

Dec. 12, 1827 - Deposition of Martin Graft who has known John and Elizabeth Gochenour upwards of fifteen years. They "lived together as man and wife until about four years ago, when the said John Gochenour deserted his said wife, and continued absent from her habitation from that time hitherto, without any just or reasonable cause.

Dec. 17, 1827 - Court granted Elizabeth Gochenour a divorce from her husband John Gochenour. Costs were $3.00 for the prothy.; $1.59 for the crier; $1.56 for the sheriff; and 37 1/2 for the certificate; making a total cost of $6.43 1/2.

Lancaster Co., Pa., Appearance Docket Nov. Term 1827 #39 - Mary Smith by her next friend, Henry Christine, vs. John Smith, libel in divorce. Sheriff reported it took him fifteen miles to serve the subpoena on John Smith. Original documents in this file are now missing.

Lancaster Co., Pa., Appearance Docket Jan. Term 1828 #4 - Mary Smith by her next friend, Henry Christine, vs. John Smith, libel in divorce.

Apr. 21, 1828 - On motion of Mr. Ellmaker, court appointed Thomas Dickey, Jr., Esq., to take depositions in this case. Original documents in this file are now missing which apparently included the depositions gathered for this case.

Apr. 24, 1828 - Court granted Mary Smith a divorce from her husband, John Smith. Costs were $3.84 for the prothy.; $3.00 for the atty.; $1.81 for the sheriff and $1.50 for the crier making a total cost of $10.15 which was paid to N.W. Sample, the prothy., on Apr. 25, 1828.

Lancaster Co., Pa., Appearance Docket Apr. Term 1828 #2 - David Culbertson, Jr., vs. Elizabeth Culbertson, libel in divorce.

Undated - Petition of David Culbertson, Jr., that he married on Feb. 22, 1821, in Lancaster Co., Pa., Elizabeth Patterson. She deserted him in Dec. of 1821 without any reasonable cause taking her infant child aged about three weeks with her.

Jan. 21, 1828 - Court issued a subpoena to Elizabeth Culbertson to appear in court for Apr. Term 1828 to answer the libel of her husband, David Culbertson, Jr., for a divorce. Sheriff reported that he served this subpoena and it required six miles of travel to do so.

Aug. 25, 1828 - Court appointed Daniel Moore, Esq., of the city of Lancaster, Pa., to take depositions in this case. Costs were $2.75 to proth., $.37 to the shrff., and $3.00 to the atty., a total cost of $6.12 paid to N.W. Sample, proth., Nov 19, 1828.

Lancaster Co., Pa., Appearance Docket Apr. Term 1828 #6 - Mary Smith by her next friend, Michael Greenawalt, vs. John Smith, libel in divorce.

Jan. 28, 1828 - Petition of Maria [sic] Smith by her next friend, Michael Greenawalt, before Samuel Dale, Esq. She married John Smith on April 1, 1824. He abused her by cruel and barbarous treatment and she was thereby forced to leave him on Feb. 1, 1825. Maria [sic] Smith signed her petition "by mark."

Jan. 28, 1828 - Court issued a subpeona to John Smith to appear in court to answer the libel of his wife, Mary Smith, for a divorce. Sheriff reported that he served this subpoena by copy and it took him ten miles to do this.

Jun. 18, 1828 - On motion of Mr. Champneys, the court appointed Samuel Dale, Esq., to take depositions in this case.

Aug. 14, 1828 - Deposition of Margaret Gallagher, widow, before Samuel Dale "saith the night she took sick one night before she had her child. I was there. He was in liquor. I was there the next night when she had her child. The midwife was called away and the Doctor brought and when she Mariah [sic] was delivered John Smith her husband went after the Doctor and some time in the night he returned and raged so that I was affraid [sic] to let him into the room where she lay. She lay trembling with fear. I had to let him come in to save his breaking the door or windows, some time after I left the house and was affraid [sic] to return to see her. He, John Smith, has lived apart from his wife and child to my knowledge more than three years, and to my belief has afforded them no assistance and on account of ill treatment she was compeled [sic] to leave him."

Aug. 14, 1828 - Deposition of Frederick Moyer of West Hempfield Twp., Lancaster Co., Pa., that "John Smith gave his wife Mariah [sic] Smith very bad treatment. She had verry [sic] bad usage in victuals (as) she had a scarce supply. He threatened to whip her and did whip her. When in childbed he abused her and attempted to drag her out. He was in liquor. He was a passionate man and seemed always angry with her. Nex [sic] he took the ax and went to cut up the bureau and I suspect if it had not been for me and my wife he would have done it. He said if he had cut the bureau he would go and cut a hickory and cut her as long as he could lift a hand or as long as she could stand. At another time he took the ramrod of his gun and struck her over the head, broke her comb and cut her head til [sic] the blood ran down and the mark remains on her head yet. Smith and wife lived in part of my house and every night when he would come home he would raise a disturbance. I was always affraid [sic] and when I would say anything he would swear heavy oaths that it was not my business, he would do as he pleased. I have seen her in winter without shoes. I have often thought that her life was in danger if it had not been for me and my wife's interference."

Aug. 20, 1828 - Daniel Hertzler reported that John Smith had received notice of depositions of witnesses to be held Aug. 14, 1828, but he said it was not worth while to attend.

Aug. 23, 1828 - Court granted Mary Smith a divorce from her husband, John Smith.

Lancaster Co., Pa., Appearance Docket Apr. Term 1828 #7 - Catharine Hogendobler by her next friend, Maria Friday, vs. Joseph Hogendobler, libel in divorce.

Jan. 22, 1828 - Petition of Catherine Hogendoebler [sic] before John Musselman, justice of the peace by her next friend, Maria Friday. She had married Joseph Hogendoebler [sic] in Jun. of 1819. Her husband deserted her in Jun. of 1820 without any just or reasonable cause and continued absent. Both Catherine Hogendoebler [sic] and Maria Friday signed "by mark."

Jan. 31, 1828 - Court issued a subpoena to Joseph Hogendobler to appear in court to answer the libel of his wife, Catharine Hogendobler, for a divorce. Sheriff reported he served this subpoena by copy on Mar. 19, 1828.

Apr. 21, 1828 - On motion of Mr. Evans, the court appointed John Musselman, Esq., to take depositions in this case.

Depositions of witnesses were somehow missing from this file.

Apr. 24, 1828 - Depositions of witnesses were read and the court granted Catherine Hogendobler a divorce from her husband, Joseph Hogendobler.

Costs were $3.09 for the prothy.; $3.00 for the atty.; $1.00 for the crier; and $1.00 for the sheriff making a total cost of $8.59 to which was added $1.50 for John Musselman; making a grand total cost of $10.09 which was paid to the prothy. on Sept. 24, 1835.

Lancaster Co., Pa., Appearance Docket Apr. Term 1828 #14 - Catharine McCausland by her next friend, George Leonard, vs. David McCausland, libel in divorce.

Feb. 8, 1828 - Petition of Catharine McCausland by her next friend, George Leonard. She married David McCausland about 1800. He deserted her from the time of their marriage until now and has given her no support. She has always lived in Pa. Catharine McCausland signed her name Catherine [sic] McCausland.

Feb. 8, 1828 - Court issued a subpoena to David McCausland to appear in court to answer the libel of his wife, Catharine McCausland, for a divorce. Sheriff reported he served this subpoena and it required him to travel fifteen miles and he reported he did not find David McCausland in his bailiwick. Continued to Aug. Term 1828 #9 (document missing).

From Appearance Docket Nov. 20, 1828 - Court appointed John Mathoit, Esq., to take depositions in this case.

Nov. 29, 1828 - Depositions read and Catharine McCausland granted a divorce from her husband, David McCausland.

Lancaster Co., Pa., Appearance Docket Apr. Term 1828 #39 - Henry Shoff vs. Susanna Shoff, libel in divorce.

Mar. 18, 1828 - Petition of Henry Shoff of Manor Twp., Lancaster Co., Pa. He married his present wife Susanna on May 28, 1824. She deserted him on May 2, 1825. He had "demeaned himself towards his said wife as a kind and affectionate husband and never by his conduct gave her any reason for withdrawing from his house."

Mar. 18, 1825 - Court issued a subpoena to Susanna Shoff to appear in court to answer the libel of her husband, Henry Shoff, for a divorce. Sheriff reported that he served this subpoena by copy and it required six miles to travel to do so.

Apr. 30, 1828 - On motion of Mr. Montgomery, the court appointed Nathaniel Lightner, Esq., to take depositions in this case.

Surname Index

ADAMS, 25
ALBERTS, 34
ALBRIGHT, 9 70 71
ANDERSON, 19
ANDREWS, 73
APP, 6 8 9 10
ARCHER, 29
ARMSTRONG, 16
ARNDT, 20.25
ARTHUR, 71
ASH, 4
ATLEE, 2
AUWERTER, 95
AXER, 40 41
AYERS, 91
AYRES, 91
BACHMAN, 83 89 92 94 98-102
    105 108 111
BACKENSTONE, 97
BACKENSTOSE, 49 97
BADER, 25-27
BADGER, 99 100
BAILIE, 110
BAINDER, 113 115
BAKER, 7 21 29 58 71
BAKESTOSE, 10
BALMER, 117
BANNER, 44
BARBER, 74 84
BARCLAY, 32
BARE, 31
BARKER, 21 23 119
BARKMAN, 46
BARR, 33 34 96 97 115
BARRETT, 106 108-110
BARTER, 23
BARTLE, 72 73

BARTON, 32 47 48 50 119
BASSLER, 96 97
BAUER, 44 45
BAUMAN, 79
BAUSMAN, 19 22 24 83
BAXTER, 25
BEAR, 9 27 67 94 95 117
BEAUSMAN, 24
BECHARD, 90
BECHERD, 90
BECKER, 44
BECKERD, 90
BEELOR, 76
BEILER, 42
BEIXLER, 5
BENDER, 28 113
BENNETT, 9
BIEGHART, 96
BINELY, 118
BITTERMAN, 118 119
BLACK, 25 73 75 76
BLOCK, 73
BOGGS, 33
BOHMER, 87
BONNET, 37-40
BOOT, 88 89
BOWER, 45
BOWMILLER, 106
BOYD, 78
BOYLES, 86
BRACKERMAN, 96
BRADERLY, 89
BRADEY, 113 115
BRADY, 113 116
BRANT, 113-115
BRATTON, 17
BREG, 74

BRENDLE, 25 29
BRENIZER, 59
BRENNEMAN, 86
BRENNIMAN, 24
BRINKLEY, 9
BRITZ, 36
BROCKE, 80
BROCKEY, 80
BROWN, 81
BRUA, 30
BUCHANAN, 50
BURD, 24
BURDEN, 91 92
BURGART, 27-29
BURK, 34 35
BURKE, 34
BURKERT, 27 28
BURKHART, 27 28
BUSH, 49
CAIN, 81 82
CALEY, 82 83
CARPENTER, 5 11 30 43 52 54
    60-64 68-70 72-74 86 119
CARTER, 101
CHAMBERS, 7
CHAMPNEY, 89 92
CHAMPNEYS, 105 122
CHAPNEY, 90
CHEW, 83
CHILD, 42 45 110
CHILDS, 46
CHRIST, 94
CHRISTINE, 121
CLARK, 3 7 84 85
CLICKNER, 117
CLUNIE, 3 4
CLYDE, 83 87
COCHRAN, 18 19 46
COIL, 51
COLIER, 3
COLP, 111 115
COLVERMAN, 11
CONLEY, 76
CONNAL, 82
CONNELLY, 75
CONWELL, 15
CORDES, 80
CORRELL, 52

CRAWFORD, 9 15 16 100
CROMMELL, 40
CROSBY, 92
CULBERTSON, 121
DALE, 59 82 84 85 87 89 91 92
    96 97 101 103 104 106 111
    117 118 121 122
DAVIS, 35 42 90
DEAN, 9
DESSINGER, 81
DETRICH, 117
DETRICK, 117
DICKEY, 110 121
DIETRICH, 78 117
DIETRICK, 117
DIFFENDERFER, 39 40
DILLER, 12
DOAK, 85
DOCHTERMAN, 47
DOKE, 85
DONNELLY, 108
DORWALT, 95
DORWART, 89 90
DOWNEY, 73 96
DOYLE, 115 116
DUNN, 96
DYER, 36 37
EAGLE, 110
EARHART, 112-115
EBERLEIN, 82
EBERMAN, 41 53 73 74
EBY, 36
ECHLER, 49
ECKERT, 61 62
ECKMAN, 120
EDWARDS, 109
EGGERT, 101
EHLER, 49 74
EICHOLTZ, 31
ELDER, 4
ELLEBERGER, 37
ELLIOTT, 87
ELLMAKER, 92 95 104 121
ENDRESS, 106
ENGLE, 43-45
ERB, 98
ERHART, 111 115
ERISMAN, 94

ESHELMAN, 57 91
ESHLEMAN, 55
ETTER, 2 93
EVANS, 100 101 123
FAHNESTOCK, 117
FALEY, 24
FERREE, 100
FISHER, 22 99 100 111
FLAGLE, 2
FLEMING, 101
FOLEY, 24
FOLTZ, 21
FOOES, 49
FORD, 28 29
FORDNEY, 23 24 37 38 94
FORNER, 9
FORNEY, 66 68-72
FOSTER, 18 19 88
FOULKE, 9
FOWLER, 110
FRANKFORD, 74
FRANKLIN, 62 99 111 115
FRANTZ, 3
FRAZEE, 46
FRAZER, 61 67 96 103 118
FRAZIER, 118
FREEMAN, 78
FREYMER, 22
FRICK, 9
FRIDAY, 122 123
FRIEL, 77
FUHRMAN, 15 79
FULLER, 108
FULTON, 4
FUNK, 32
GALBRAETH, 64
GALBRAITH, 65
GALLACHER, 16 17
GALLAGHER, 122
GALLEGHER, 57
GALLIGHER, 56
GALT, 25
GAMBLE, 7 8
GANTZ, 92 104
GARMAN, 104
GARRETSON, 88
GAYLORD, 42
GEISE, 40

GEITER, 53
GELTMACHER, 87
GERBER, 47
GETTMACHER, 86 87
GETZ, 67 68 94
GIBBONS, 106 108
GIBSON, 91
GIDDENS, 49 50
GILBERT, 119 120
GILLMORE, 95
GILMORE, 95
GLONINGER, 14 34
GOCHENAUER, 78 117
GOCHENOUR, 120 121
GOSS, 73
GRACIOUS, 58 59
GRAEFF, 7
GRAFF, 13
GRAFT, 120
GRAHAMS, 3
GRAYBILL, 92 93
GRAYSON, 1 3
GREBILL, 117
GREEN, 35
GREENAWALT, 121
GREER, 8
GRIER, 22
GRIMES, 74
GROSE, 106
GROSS, 9
GRUBB, 48 49
GRUBE, 98
GUYOR, 21
HACKLEROTH, 21 22
HAGER, 9
HAGEY, 10
HAINES, 22 30 53 85 88 93 111
HAINS, 30
HALL, 64
HAMBRIGHT, 47 49 59 96 97
HAMILTON, 100 101
HAMMOND, 32
HARKINS, 51 52
HARMAN, 25
HARRIS, 2-4
HARTLEY, 94
HARTMAN, 30 31
HARTUNG, 16

HASSELBACH, 38
HASTON, 102
HAUCK, 105 106
HAUFFMAN, 10
HAUK, 105
HAWMAN, 70
HEBERLING, 92
HECK, 25
HECKERT, 120
HEISS, 48 49 117 118
HELLER, 5 96
HEMPFIELD, 87
HENBERGER, 20
HENRY, 9 10 18 19 29
HERBST, 61
HERNLEY, 48
HERR, 11 37 88
HERSHEY, 101 102
HERTZLER, 105 122
HESS, 28 52
HESTAN, 65 66
HESTON, 64
HEWTER, 16
HIBSCHMAN, 81
HILL, 57
HINKLE, 50
HIPPLE, 20
HISTAN, 64
HOAR, 90
HOCK, 112
HODGES, 57
HOEFFERT, 86
HOFF, 36 41 45 53 59 67
HOFFMAN, 85 100 119
HOFFMEUR, 75
HOFFMYER, 75
HOGENDOBLER, 122 123
HOGENDOEBLER, 123
HOHWERTER, 44
HOKE, 15
HOLLIDAY, 71
HOLLINGER, 86
HOPKINS, 17 46 50 62 64 70
    103
HOSS, 28
HUBER, 36
HUBLEY, 2 5-7 10-12
HUDSON, 90 91

HUGHS, 53
HUMMELL, 47
HUTCHIN, 18 19
HUTCHISON, 4
IMHEL, 77
ISRAEL, 16
JACKSON, 44
JACOBS, 95 98
JENKINS, 10 90 100
JOHENS, 96
JOHN, 28
JOHNSON, 79
JOHNSTON, 116
JONES, 54 55 75 80
JORDAN, 10
KAHN, 12
KAIN, 29
KAINES, 24
KANE, 102 103
KARCH, 10
KAUFFMAN, 14 15 24 102 117
    118
KAUFMAN, 42 74
KEAN, 2
KEEF, 19-21
KEENER, 48
KEHLER, 30
KELHAEFFER, 56
KELHAEFLER, 55
KELHEFFER, 56
KELKER, 2
KELLER, 1 72 73 85 106
KELLHEFFER, 53 54
KELLY, 76 77 81 108
KENDIG, 117
KENDRICK, 6
KESLER, 58 59
KILE, 44 45
KILLIAN, 109
KING, 13
KLAPPER, 34
KLAUS, 34
KLEIN, 62-64
KLIE, 44
KLINE, 44 62 64-66
KNOWLE, 57
KOEHM, 83 84
KOENIG, 53

KOHL, 23
KOLP, 111 112
KREIDER, 9
KUBNOR, 26
KUHN, 5 10 11
LAMBERT, 72 73
LANDIS, 109
LAWMASE, 71
LEAMAN, 12
LEAMON, 11-13
LECHLER, 37-39
LEFEVER, 9
LEHNART, 43
LEIBLEN, 85
LEIBLIN, 74
LEIBLY, 10 63 85
LENHART, 44
LEONARD, 123
LIBBEY, 58
LICK, 2
LIEBLY, 63
LIGGETT, 20
LIGHT, 22 24 33 43 49 67 70-72 74 77
LIGHTER, 43
LIGHTNER, 95-97 100 101 103 124
LIND, 62
LINDY, 103
LINK, 1
LIONS, 41 42
LITHGOE, 59
LITHGOW, 59
LLOYD, 43
LOCHLER, 9
LOMASE, 72
LOMAX, 71 72
LONG, 10 11 13 14 79 84 87 90 116
LOVETT, 40
LOWE, 119
LOWELL, 47
LOWMASE, 71
LUBY, 62
LUTZ, 99
LYNE, 119
MAGAWEN, 76
MARKLEY, 53 119

MART, 90
MARTIN, 17 19 25 31 35 48 83 94 104 105
MATHIOT, 84 97 103 105 117 120
MATHOIT, 123
MATTER, 33 43 73 75 76 87
MAURER, 116
MAWER, 62 63 66
MAY, 104
MAYER, 6 14 15
MAYERS, 64
MCCALLISTER, 24
MCCAMANT, 91
MCCARRON, 114 115
MCCASLAND, 29 30
MCCAUSLAND, 123
MCCLEARY, 3
MCCLURE, 51
MCCONNELL, 13
MCCORMICK, 1
MCCOY, 8 9
MCCULLOUGH, 8 9 110
MCDILL, 17
MCDONALD, 87-90
MCENTIRE, 8 76
MCFADDIEN, 24
MCGLAUCHLIN, 34
MCGOVERN, 77
MCKEAN, 1 2
MCKINNEY, 117
MCKNIGHT, 111
MCNAUGHTON, 108
MCNEAL, 84
MEARING, 118
MEIXEL, 99
MEIXIL, 99
MELNOR, 27
MENOLD, 103
METZGAR, 10
MEYLIN, 60
MICHAEL, 43 68 69
MICHAN, 64
MIGHTEN, 64
MILES, 25
MILLER, 6 10 20 24 36 37 42 43 45 69 73 79 82 85 117
MILNERS, 26

MILNOR, 26 27
MILNORS, 27
MONTGOMERY, 1 3 26 32 124
MOORE, 77 78 80 84-90 95 97
    120 121
MORRISON, 8 13 95 97
MOSHER, 57 58
MOURER, 115 116
MOYER, 122
MUCHLENBERG, 6
MUHLENBERG, 2 7 22 23 79 84
    87 90 92
MUHLENBERGER, 83
MULL, 120
MUSSELLMAN, 123
MUSSELMAN, 123
MUSSENTINE, 16
MUSSER, 102 103
MYER, 9 14 44
MYERS, 65 66
NACE, 60-62
NAGLE, 45 46
NAUMAN, 35
NEALE, 99 100
NEFF, 67 75
NERS, 45
NEWCOMMER, 40
NICHOLAS, 92 93
NICHOLASON, 49
NICHOLS, 32
NICHOLSON, 50
NISLEY, 117
NOECKLY, 99
NORTH, 35
O'HOGAN, 19 20
ODERWALD, 22 23
ODERWALT, 23
OLIVER, 17
ORDWALD, 23
OVERHALTZER, 98
OVERHOLZER, 98
OYER, 9 35
PAIN, 6
PAINE, 6
PAINTER, 5
PASSMORE, 75
PATRICK, 51 52
PATTER, 26

PATTERSON, 58 85 86 121
PAUGLE, 104 105
PAYRES, 91
PEDEN, 35
PEELOR, 77
PENROSE, 12
PERRY, 59 60
PERSON, 7
PORTER, 61 62 64 68 88 94
POWELL, 117
RAHM, 19
RANK, 46 47
RATHFON, 95 96
RAWLINS, 73
REA, 33
REIGART, 13 17 21 26 28 30 97
REIGARTS, 98
REIHM, 33
REINHART, 48 49
REIST, 10
REITZEL, 19 21 23 85 94
REPLEY, 57
REPLY, 56
RHEA, 33
RICHARDSON, 111-116
RIDDLE, 41 42
RINE, 13 17 19 21
RINHEHART, 117
RINZ, 11
ROAN, 7
ROBINSON, 16 76 98 99
ROCK, 83
ROFF, 89
ROGERS, 43
ROHRER, 115
ROLAND, 11 12 104
ROSS, 34 38-40 45 53 70 105
ROTH, 66 68 69
ROY, 101
RUCH, 77 78
RUDY, 5 30
RUPLEY, 67
RUPLY, 70
RUTTER, 13
SAMPLE, 94 95 98-102 104 105
    108 111 115 118 121
SAUNDERS, 73
SCHLENKER, 99

SCHWENK, 87
SCOTT, 8
SECHRIST, 97
SEELEY, 92
SEGER, 12
SEGLESMITH, 48 49
SELLARS, 97
SELSER, 2
SERGISON, 91
SHAFFNER, 36 93
SHALLAH, 102
SHARER, 69
SHAUM, 10
SHEET, 35
SHEFFER, 15
SHELLER, 53 64 66
SHELLY, 33
SHENK, 15
SHERER, 60
SHERICK, 42
SHERKS, 87
SHIFFER, 44 45
SHINDEL, 94
SHIPPEN, 1
SHIRK, 46 47
SHOENEBERGER, 42
SHOFF, 123 124
SHONEBERGER, 42
SHREINER, 6 7
SHRINER, 6 77 78
SHRIVER, 60-62
SHULTZ, 61 62
SHUMAN, 49
SIMONY, 1
SINGHAAS, 6 7
SINGHORSE, 7
SITES, 6
SIVENTZELL, 10
SLAYMAKER, 102
SMALL, 99
SMITH, 18 19 21 24 34 38 46 61
    77 79 86 97 98 100 121 122
SMOCK, 39
SNEBELY, 27 28
SNYDER, 29 94
SOMMERS, 109 110
SPEALMAN, 61 62
SPEAR, 82 101

SPROAT, 40
STAUFFER, 5 9 35 36 104
STEADY, 100
STEELE, 19
STELEY, 82
STICKEL, 75
STINEMAN, 9
STOCKSLEGGER, 83
STOGDEN, 92
STOHLER, 1
STONE, 90
STONER, 77
STORMBACH, 103
STORRICK, 78
STOUFFER, 52
STREET, 35
STREINER, 10
STRENGE, 102
STUFFT, 9
SUMMYS, 98
SWEITZEL, 85
TATE, 35
TAYLOR, 33
TEMPLETON, 111
TERMINER, 35
TEURTAC, 38
TEURTOR, 39
TEURTOY, 39
THOMAS, 71 72 110
THOMPSON, 9 10 17-19
THORNBURG, 7
TILLOTSON, 31
TOME, 14
TRINQUE, 76
TURNER, 9
TUTTLE, 18 19
UHRICH, 79
ULERICH, 10
UNDERWOOD, 47
URBAN, 105 106
USNER, 96
VARNES, 111
VONKENEN, 29
VONKENIN, 27 28
WAGGONER, 9
WAGGONNER, 9
WAGNER, 9
WALLACE, 18 19 96

WALLICK, 64 65
WATKINS, 7
WATSON, 64 65
WEAVER, 86 87
WEIDLER, 74
WEILEY, 22
WEILY, 22
WEISS, 80
WENGER, 117
WEST, 18 19
WHEN, 96 97
WHITE, 8 105
WHITEHILL, 34
WIKES, 83
WILHELM, 80
WILKINSON, 64-66
WILLY, 18 19
WILSON, 2 7 25 27 45 46 70 71
WIND, 53

WITHERS, 33
WITMER, 9
WOLF, 79
WRIGHT, 1 2 79 84 85 87 97
    102 103 111
YEATES, 5
YENTZ, 40
YORK, 95
YOUNDE, 98
YOUNDT, 98
YOUNG, 14 15 19 23 24 43
ZAHN, 120
ZANTINGER, 5
ZANTZING, 31
ZANTZINGER, 7 21 25 27 29-31
ZEHMER, 60
ZELL, 80 90 116
ZUBER, 5 6

www.ingramcontent.com/pod-product-compliance
Lightning Source LLC
Chambersburg PA
CBHW070251290326
41930CB00041B/2438